IMAGES OF ENGLAND

GRANTHAM
REVISITED

IMAGES OF ENGLAND

GRANTHAM
REVISITED

FRED LEADBETTER

Frontispiece: Multi-view postcards were just as popular with the Edwardians as they are today. After all, this Christmas greeting card dating from the early 1900s gave you seven images for the price of one.

First published in 2006 by Tempus Publishing Limited

Reprinted in 2011 by
The History Press
The Mill, Brimscombe Port,
Stroud, Gloucestershire, GL5 2QG
www.thehistorypress.co.uk

© Fred Leadbetter, 2011

The right of Fred Leadbetter to be identified as the Author of this work has been asserted in accordance with the Copyrights, Designs and Patents Act 1988.

All rights reserved. No part of this book may be reprinted or reproduced or utilised in any form or by any electronic, mechanical or other means, now known or hereafter invented, including photocopying and recording, or in any information storage or retrieval system, without the permission in writing from the Publishers.

British Library Cataloguing in Publication Data.
A catalogue record for this book is available from the British Library.

ISBN 978 0 7524 3825

Typesetting and origination by Tempus Publishing Limited.
Printed in Great Britain.

Contents

	Acknowledgements	6
	Introduction	7
	Bibliography	8
one	Approach from the South-West	9
two	Approach from the West	21
three	Into Grantham on the A52	33
four	High Street and Castlegate Area	41
five	St Peter's Hill Area	55
six	The London Road and New Somerby Area	73
seven	Into Grantham on the A607	91
eight	Westgate and the Market Place	103
nine	The Vine Street to Manthorpe Road Area	111
ten	Out on the A607	119

Acknowledgements

I would like to take this opportunity to thank all the people who have in some way contributed to the compilation of this book; this includes the many people over the years that have been willing to share with me their knowledge of local events and give life and meaning to many of the images contained in its pages. Thanks must also go to the many local historians both past and present whose work has made mine that much easier when searching for information on our area's heritage. The staff of the Grantham Library also deserve a mention for their patience and fortitude when dealing with an amateur such as myself who, without their help, would not always look in the right place for relevant information. I must also acknowledge my wife Jen who has helped with suggestions on content and has shown patience and resilience during my tantrums with our computer. Last, but by no means least, I would like to acknowledge the local photographers whose images have come down through the years and without whose work books like this would not be possible.

Introduction

Once again it gives me great pleasure to share part of my collection of local postcards, photographs and ephemera with readers who, like myself, are fascinated and intrigued by a way of life that has now gone forever. This book contains images from the 1870s through to the early 1970s, a span of 100 years that saw parts of Grantham and its surrounding villages change, in many cases beyond all recognition. The informed reader will note that there are some omissions relating to the town's history which they may feel should have been included in this book but where I have felt that these have been covered fully in other publications I have left them out in favour of more original images that may not have been seen before.

Grantham has obtained its wealth by a variety of means over the years. In medieval times it prospered on wool from the long thick coats of its sheep which fed on the heath lands on the outskirts of the town. It has also been a centre for the tanning of leather, shoe manufacture and the curing of skins. It has seen its share of gun and watch makers; it has even been host to its own button factory. There was once a thriving wicker and cane furniture manufacturer and a very successful brewing industry with several maltings dotted around the town. Despite all of the above, and many other trades too numerous to mention here, the area around the town had always been mainly a farming community. This altered course to a great extent in the mid-1800s with the coming of the Industrial Revolution, and after being a major engineering centre for more than 150 years the town has once again moved on. Although there are still several very good light engineering companies in the area Grantham has now mainly left behind its engineering heritage and entered a new age of commerce.

Gone now are the factories that made agricultural equipment which was the envy of the world, no more are the skills required to manufacture cranes, armaments and road rollers. Today the biggest employers in the area are the food processing industry, several large supermarkets, logistics and other service industries. This is a far cry from when our forefathers would spend a long working day in the noise and grime of the town's factories and their womenfolk would set out with baskets on their arms to visit the various high street or corner shops for the family's daily needs.

Contained in the pages of this book are images which I hope will interest and entertain the reader, be they old enough to remember some of the later photographs or young enough only to discover how our town has developed into what it is today. I have not set out to write an academic history of Grantham and some of its villages, the book is merely intended to bring pleasure to the reader as he or she thumbs through its pages in moments of idle reverie.

Bibliography

White's Directories of Lincolnshire, various dates
Kelly's Directories of Lincolnshire, various dates
Palmers Almanacs, Various dates
Harrisons Almanacs, Various dates
Grantham *Red Books*, Various dates
Grantham Journal

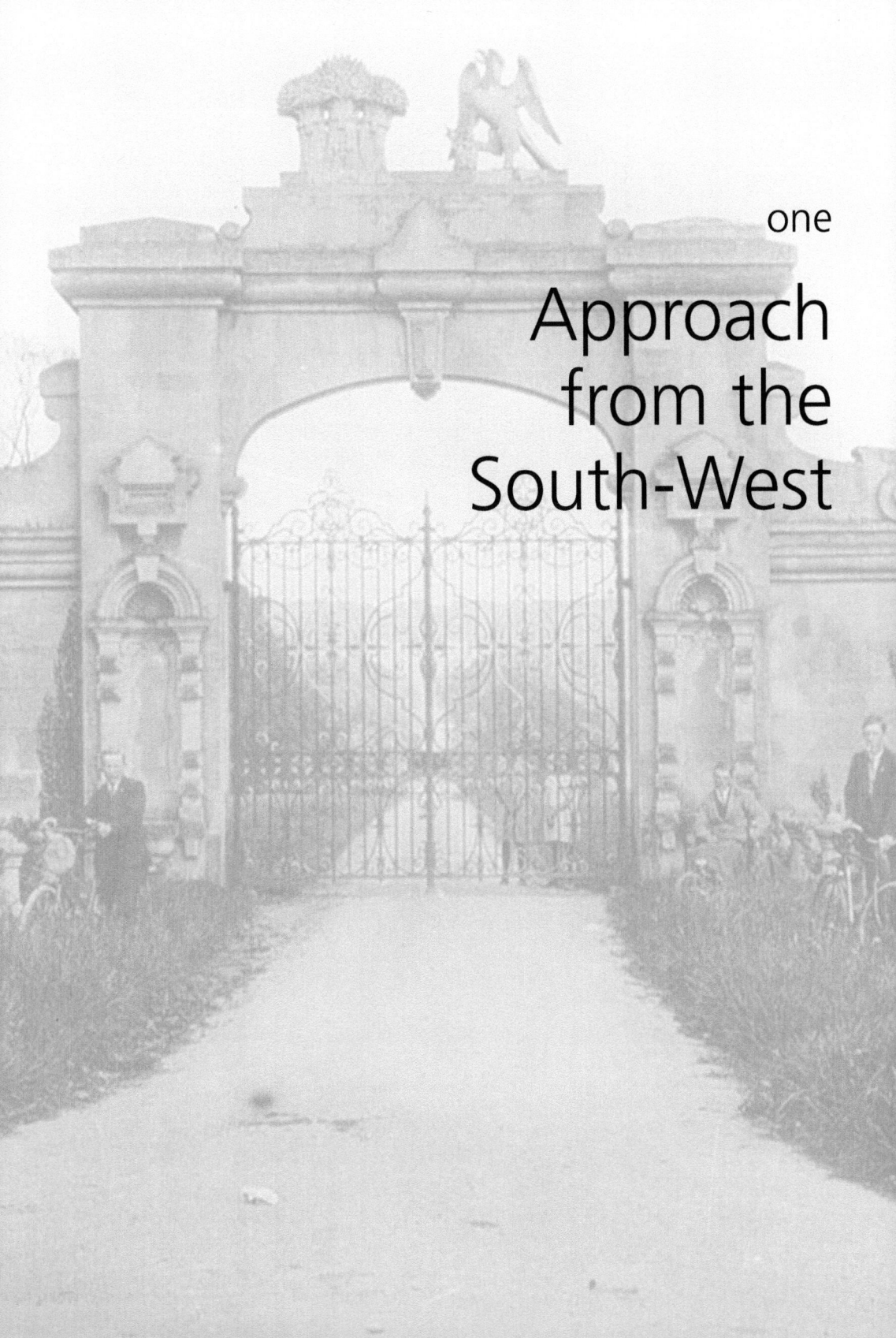

one

Approach from the South-West

Denton lies four miles south-west of Grantham on the A607 from Melton Mowbray. This printed postcard shows the descent down into the village on Main Street to the right while on the left of the view is the old Denton Manor gatehouse. The postcard was posted just after the First World War in the 1920s.

Some distance from the gatehouse inside the park were these attractive Bede Houses dating from the 1650s. Built of local ironstone they lasted over 300 years before being demolished in 1980. This card was posted from the village in 1911.

A view of the park on a postcard sent to Derbyshire in 1911. The scene looks over one of the lakes showing the drive down from the gatehouse. The old Bede Houses can be seen through the trees.

Before the First World War many of the local estates allowed the military to use their parklands for training exercises. The Welby Estate was no exception to this rule and here we see soldiers of the Leicestershire Regiment coming into camp. The card was sent by a soldier called Bob Watton who states it is only a short message as the bugle has just sounded for dress.

An aerial view of Denton Manor, home of the Welby family. There have been several manors in the village over the years: this one was built in the early 1880s from a Tudor-style design by Sir Arthur Blomfield. The manor was cruelly damaged by fire in 1906, leaving only a portion of the west side of the building intact.

On the day after the fire men from Grantham builders Rudd & Sons can be seen removing loose masonry and beginning to erect a temporary roof over the damaged building. The manor was finally demolished in the late 1930s with a major sale of fixtures and fittings taking place in February 1939.

The aftermath of a house fire on Casthorpe Road, *c.* 1910. Somewhat less spectacular than the manor fire but no doubt just as traumatic for the Johnson family, the occupants at the time. Mr Johnson had gone into the pantry with a lighted candle to fetch potatoes which he had kept on straw. The candle fell on the straw and the rest, as they say, is history. Walter Wheeler of High Street, Grantham published the card, one of his rarer photographic images.

A view of the post office on Main Street taken by Grantham photographer Alfred Emery in the early 1900s. The Geeson family ran the post office in the village from the early 1800s until it closed in 1991. Before moving to Main Street the post office was in premises at the west end of Church Street. The letter box can still be seen, bricked up in the wall. The Geesons later produced many good-quality postcards of the village.

In Morris's Directory of Lincolnshire for 1863 it states that William Tinkler was the publican of the Welby Arms, Denton. This view, some sixty or so years later, gives an impression of a tranquil village scene, difficult to imitate in this age of hustle and bustle.

The Denton School football team of 1927 and a very determined bunch they look. From left to right, back row: W. Everton, R. Everton, V. Newman, N. Bentley. Middle row: F. Doughty, R. Scoffield, P. Humphries, A. Bullimore, L. Lee. Front row: G. Pinder, S. Short.

These youngsters patiently pose for the photographer before tucking in to the village's annual Band of Hope Picnic Feast. The date on the board is 22 September 1908, and their mothers have turned them out in their Sunday best for the occasion.

The village of Harlaxton lies three miles from Grantham on the A607 from Melton Mowbray. This fine set of gates off the main road leads down a mile-long drive to Harlaxton Manor, home to the Gregory family until the late 1930s. When Major Phillip Pearson-Gregory inherited the manor in 1935 he decided to sell the property and, on 28 September 1937, the whole estate was disposed of at auction.

The impressive façade of Harlaxton Manor on a postcard, *c.* 1910. Building began in the 1830s when the incumbent squire, Gregory Gregory, commissioned architect Anthony Salvin to build his dream out of Ancaster stone. However the two men had their differences and once Salvin had completed the exterior in 1837 he was replaced by William Burn, who is credited with much of the interior. The manor was finally completed in 1855. At the time of writing the building is occupied by the University of Evansville.

A view of High Street looking up towards the A607 taken in the first quarter of the 1900s. Several trees and hedges now hide this view to a great extent but apart from the odd conservatory and some in-filling it has changed little over the years.

A postcard of the obelisk and village green, also from the early 1900s. The fork in the road to the rear of the obelisk has now been filled in and modern-day traffic would perhaps require the children posing here for the photographer to take greater care when crossing the road.

When this scene in Church Street was taken sometime between the wars, the house on the right, now a private residence, was the village post office. The post office had moved around the village over the twentieth century. In Kelly's directory for 1909 the sub-postmaster was Joseph Pickworth. He was also the local baker and his shop was at No. 22 High Street, next to what is now the village store. Later it moved to Woodbine Cottage and after the house in this view it moved over the road in Church Street before finally settling in its present position on the corner of Pond Street and High Street.

Another view of Church Street, this time looking down towards the village green. The card dates from the first decade of the 1900s.

The farm and school with the church of St Mary and St Peter in the background was a very popular scene for local Edwardian postcard publishers. This photographic card gives a nice clear image of the buildings.

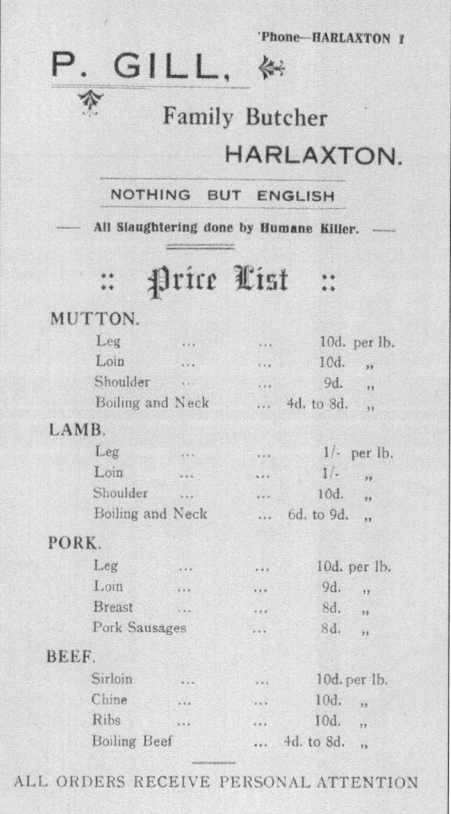

Above: Many communities today have lost their village ponds. Harlaxton still has one at the top of Pond Street and has kept it in good order. Today it is the home of much wildlife, including a colony of ducks.

Left: I'm not sure if the animals in the above view belonged to Percy Gill the butcher, but if they did, then they would have ended up in his shop which was on Church Street near where the village hall now stands. Issued in the 1930s, the cost of the meat on this price list would be very popular with today's housewives.

two

Approach from the West

Bottesford lies seven miles from Grantham just over the Lincolnshire border in Leicestershire. This view of the High Street was posted in 1956 when the A52 from Nottingham still ran through the village.

The roadway in Albert Street is wider now than when this postcard was published by Needham Brothers of Grantham around 1910, but the thoroughfare still retains some of its attractive grass verges.

The caption on this card states 'road improvement at Bottesford', but this view from the early 1900s looking down Belvoir Road surely didn't have the bypass, opened in 1989, in mind. The shop on the right, now a private residence, was a cycle shop when this photograph was taken, one of many that appeared in Edwardian England to cater for the ever-increasing popularity of this mode of transport.

It looks as though all the children of the village have turned out for this scene near the village cross and stocks. The card was issued by William Samuel in the 1920s and sold from his shop in Market Street. His premises can be seen to the left of the cross with an advert for Colman's Mustard on the wall.

A view from around 1910 of the cross, stocks, and whipping post from the opposite angle, looking down Market Street. The man on the tricycle in the background peddles past the Bull Hotel, one of the village pubs. The stocks and whipping post were resited to the left of the cross in the 1960s.

Another of the village's public houses is the Rutland Arms on the High Street. When this advertising card was sent in 1908 the publican, John William Cooper, must have been a very busy chap. Not only did he brew his own beer on site, he was involved in arranging sightseeing excursions from Nottingham for Belvoir Castle and his pub was also the headquarters of the Bottesford Angling Club.

The River Devon runs through the village and these two gentlemen pursuing the piscatorial art probably bought their angling tickets from John at the Rutland Arms. The photograph was taken by F. Taylor of Queen Street and is dated on the back 27 July 1914.

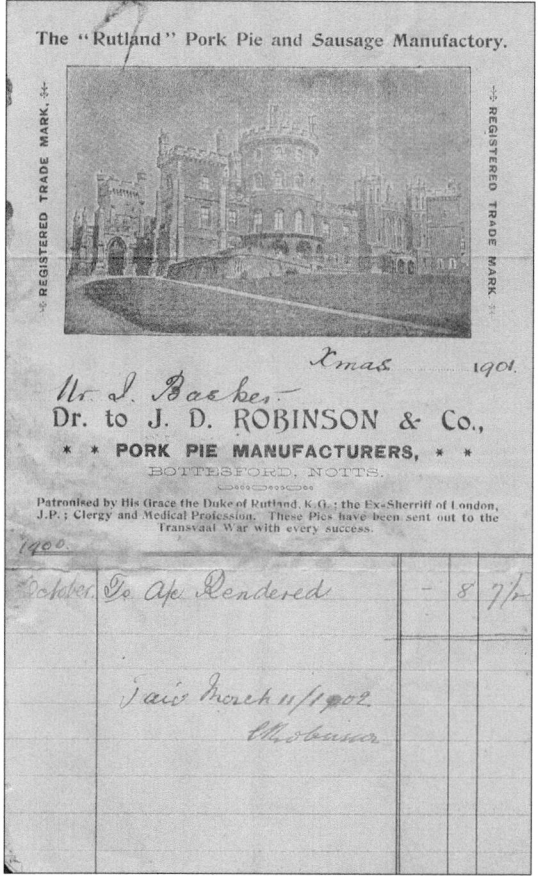

Above: A scene looking down Castle View Road, Easthorpe, a hamlet close to Bottesford. The card is another produced by William Samuel in the 1920s and sold from his shop in Market Street.

Left: The Duke of Rutland must have been keen on John Robinson's pork pies to allow him to use a view of his castle on the butcher's billheads. John, whose shop was in Market Street, also quotes the ex-Sheriff of London among his customers and states that his pies have been sent to the Transvaal with every success. I'm sure the soldiers fighting the Boers in Africa found them very welcome.

After the Battle of Hastings it was William the Conqueror's standard bearer, Robert de Todeni, who built the first castle on this site and called it Belvoir (beautiful view). It has been the home of the Duke of Rutland's family for over 500 years. The view from the castle overlooking the vale is no less beautiful today than it was to those Norman knights almost 1,000 years ago.

The Peacock Hotel was very close to the castle and did a roaring trade with the tourists who came first by horse and carriage and later, as in this view from the early 1920s, by car and charabanc. The hotel closed many years ago and the building is now a private residence called Belvoir Lodge.

The village of Barrowby lies approximately two miles from Grantham just off the A52. The church of All Saints dates from the thirteenth century, but like many of our village churches is probably built on the site of an earlier place of worship.

George Earle-Welby was rector of the parish from 1849-1900 and the lychgate to the churchyard, seen here on a postcard looking down Church Street around 1905, was erected to celebrate the golden wedding of Cannon Welby and his wife in 1895.

Another view of Church Street about the same date, taken from the junction of Main Street, High Road and Rectory Lane. This image, published by Needham Bros of Grantham, shows the Reading Room which was presented to the village in 1899 by Cannon Welby in remembrance of over fifty years as rector of the parish.

A scene in High Road from the first quarter of the 1900s. The White Swan public house stands at the junction with Main Street and still serves the community as it has done for nearly 200 years. White's Directory of 1842 gives the publican as Thomas Nelson. Behind the lamp-post standing close to the entrance to Chapel Lane can be seen the premises that are now the present-day post office.

Main Street from the other direction on a much earlier postcard, posted in 1908. It not only gives a closer view of the Marquis of Granby but also shows, on the right, the site of the village post office at the turn of the nineteenth century. Kelly's Directory for 1908 gives the sub-postmistress as Mrs Ada Annie Beel. The premises were later to become a butcher's shop run by Samuel Griffin. The property was sold to Skinners in the 1950s and they continued their business on this site until building new premises nearby.

Opposite above: Main Street in the 1950s when the village still had two public houses. The White Swan is on the extreme left and the sign for the Marquis of Granby can be seen further down the street. The latter closed in 1959 and the building is now a private house. The wall still surrounds the village green in this view; cattle were once left to graze here until led across the road, through the gate on the corner to the slaughter house opposite.

Right: This windmill was situated on Casthorpe Road down Mill Lane. It was erected by the Swallow family in around 1870 and worked until the second decade of the 1900s when Frank Swallow decided to concentrate his business on his two Grantham sites.

Below: Another view of the mill, this time showing the chimney linked to an oven which was used to dry off damp grain before presenting it to the millstones.

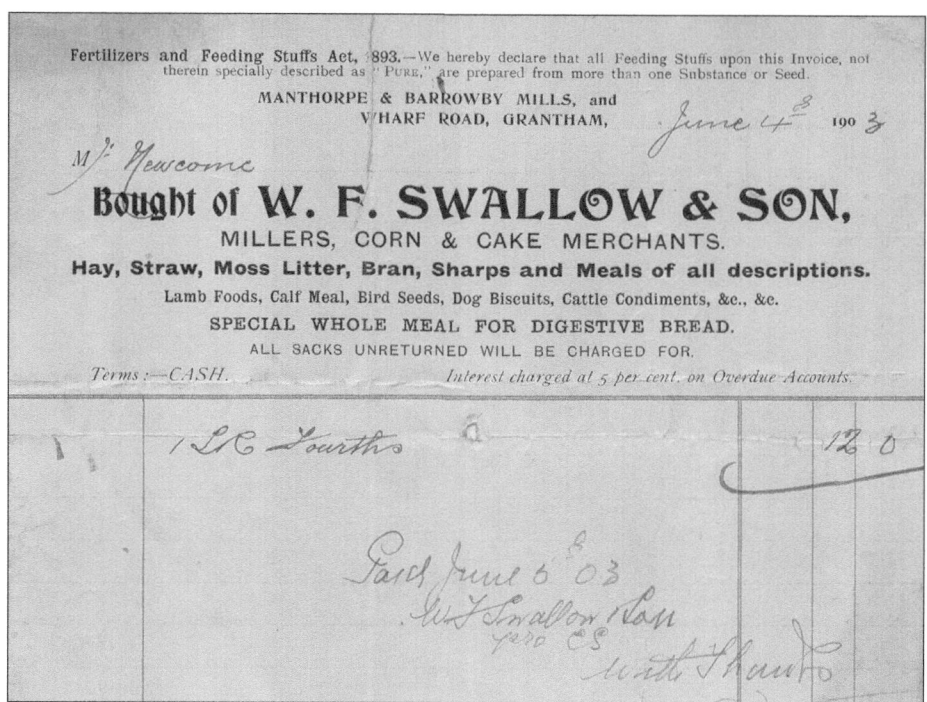

A bill-head dated June 1903 stating the location of the three sites from which the Swallow business operated at the turn of the century – Manthorpe and Barrowby Mills and offices at No. 4 Wharf Road.

Barrowby has seen many changes in the last 100 years but apart from a few minor alterations this view of Low Road remains much the same as when the photograph was taken around 1920. The Grange, which can be seen middle right in the photograph, is one of the village's oldest remaining buildings with a date of 1656 on one of its original walls.

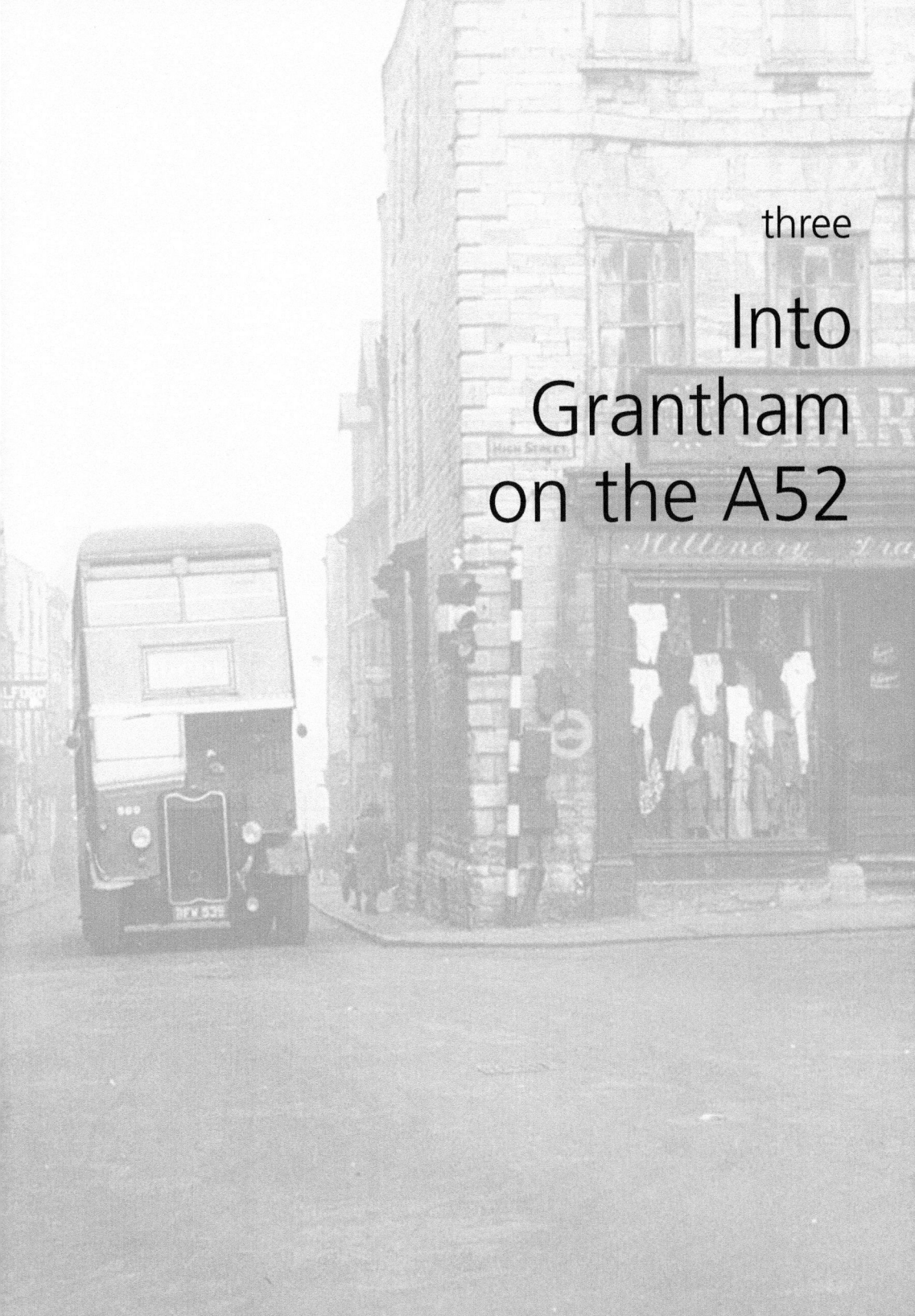

three

Into Grantham on the A52

A printed card from the early 1900s showing the descent into Grantham down Barrowby Road towards the railway bridge. The pathway in this view looks almost as wide as the road, with a large expanse of grass separating the two.

Looking up towards the railway bridge on Barrowby Road on a postcard dated 1918. Today the bridge and the grand town houses on the right of the scene are all that are recognisable after extensive road improvements have taken place to try and ensure a steady flow of traffic through the town.

Right: A quiet view in North Street in the early years of the 1900s. The Blue Bell public house stood on the corner at the junction to Barrowby Road for approximately 200 years until it was demolished in the 1990s to make way for a new road system and a supermarket car park. The motor works on the left of the view belonged to James Smith, one of the town's first motor engineers. Note the tree growing in the road, a poignant reminder of Grantham's arboreal past.

Below: In 1896 James Smith had a hardware business in North Street and by 1900 he was manufacturing bicycles in Brownlow Street. He was one of the first local engineers to grasp the significance of the coming age of the motor car and by 1905 he had opened these works at No. 13 North Street.

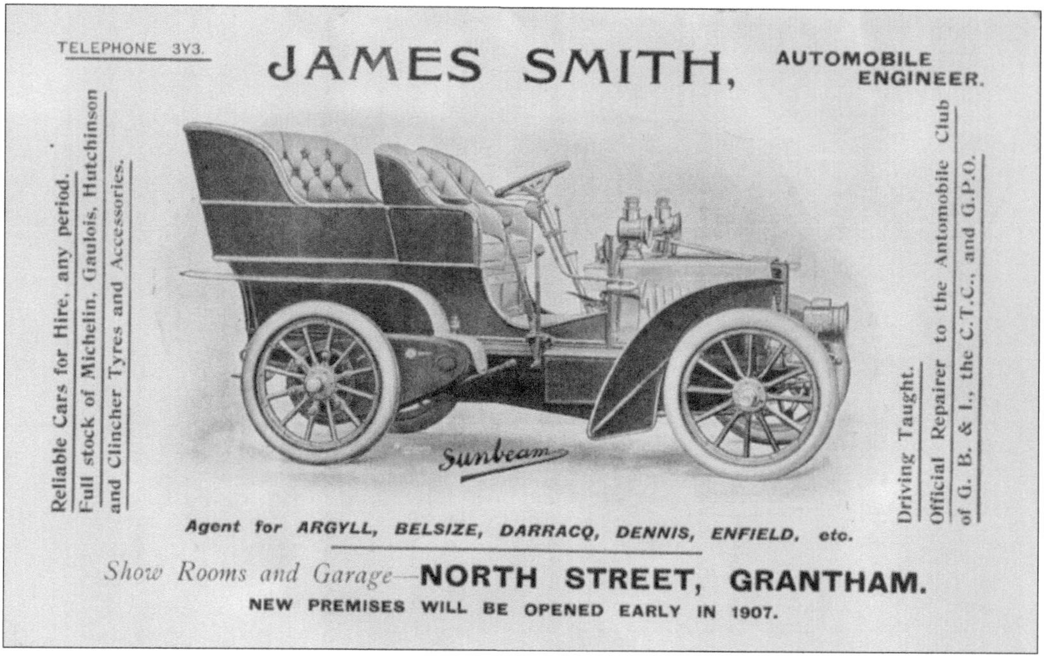
TELEPHONE 3Y3.
JAMES SMITH,
AUTOMOBILE ENGINEER.
Reliable Cars for Hire, any period.
Full stock of Michelin, Gaulois, Hutchinson and Clincher Tyres and Accessories.
Sunbeam
Driving Taught.
Official Repairer to the Automobile Club of G. B. & I., the C.T.C., and G.P.O.
Agent for ARGYLL, BELSIZE, DARRACQ, DENNIS, ENFIELD, etc.
Show Rooms and Garage—NORTH STREET, GRANTHAM.
NEW PREMISES WILL BE OPENED EARLY IN 1907.

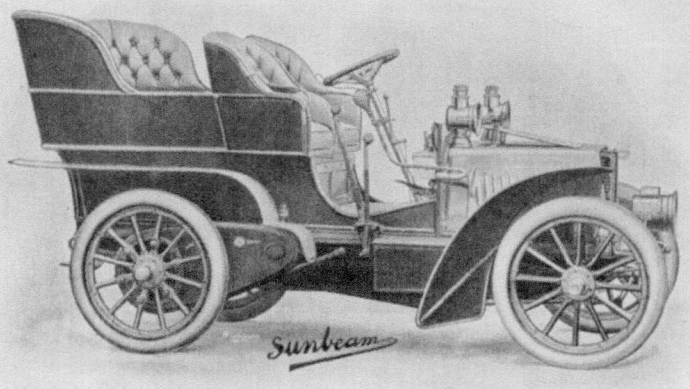

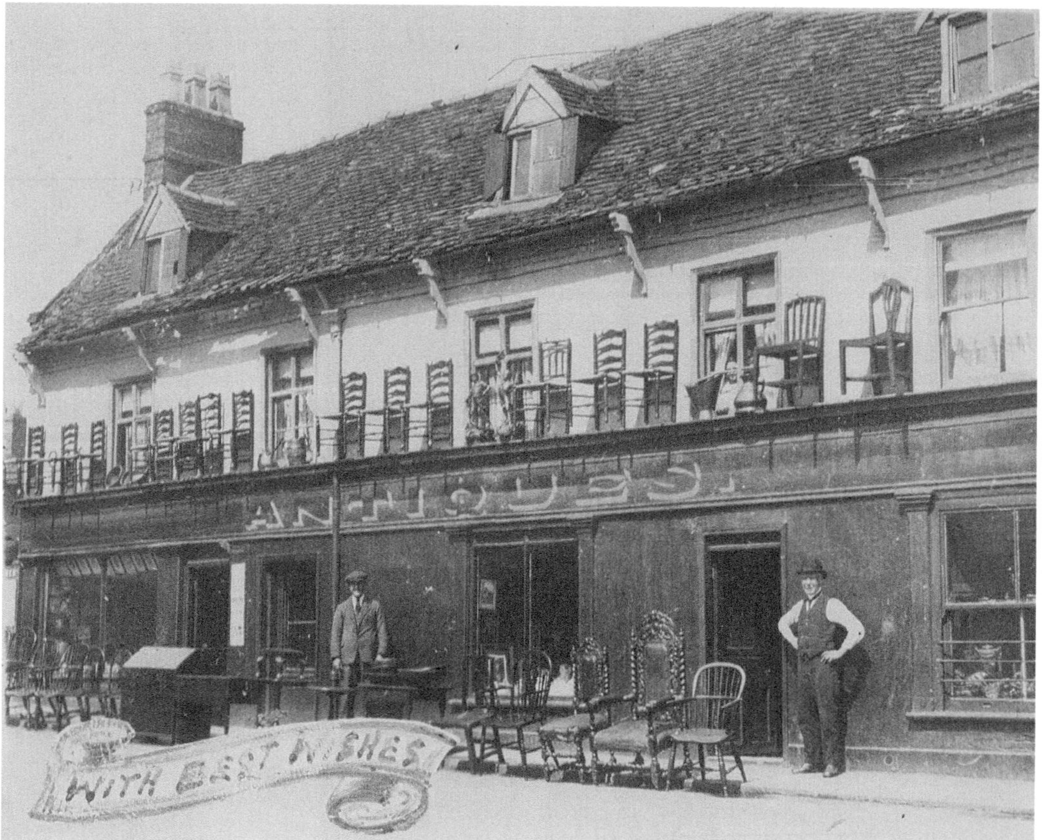
ANTIQUES
WITH BEST WISHES

WATER GATE, GRANTHAM (1)

Above: The bottom of Watergate in 1947. Most of the buildings in this view have now succumbed to the march of progress, including the tallest of them all that dominates the scene. This was the home of Harrison's, who manufactured wicker furniture and willow goods which included children's perambulators, wash baskets etc. William Brewster Harrison established the firm in the mid-1800s and was an influential personage in the town, becoming mayor in 1894.

Right: A catalogue for Harrison's products dating from the late 1800s. The company's works were behind the shop in Union Street and they had osier beds up Dysart Road and along the canal on Harlaxton Road. The 'Willows' were always a favourite spot for local fishermen to try their luck.

Opposite above: An advertisement for James's North Street business from a local publication of 1906. As can be seen along the bottom he was already looking to expand and modernise.

Opposite below: In 1919 Thomas B. Cooper had an antique business in Elmer Street South. By 1925 he had moved to these premises at Nos 1 and 2 Chapel Street, situated at the bottom of Watergate. He took over the shop from the Grantham People's Supply Co. Society Ltd. This view dates from 1933 and was taken by George Scothern, a local photographer who at the time lived close by at No. 5 Chapel Street. The shop was demolished in the early 1950s.

Opposite above: When this scene was captured on camera just after the Second World War Watergate was still part of the Great North Road. On a somewhat misty morning traffic slowly wends its way up towards the High Street.

Opposite below: An earlier view of Watergate dating from the 1920s. Cooper's antique shop can be seen across the bottom of the street. The site is now occupied by part of the Premier Court development. After the Second World War it was decided to widen the road and demolition of all the buildings on the right of the scene began in the late 1940s and continued into the early 1960s.

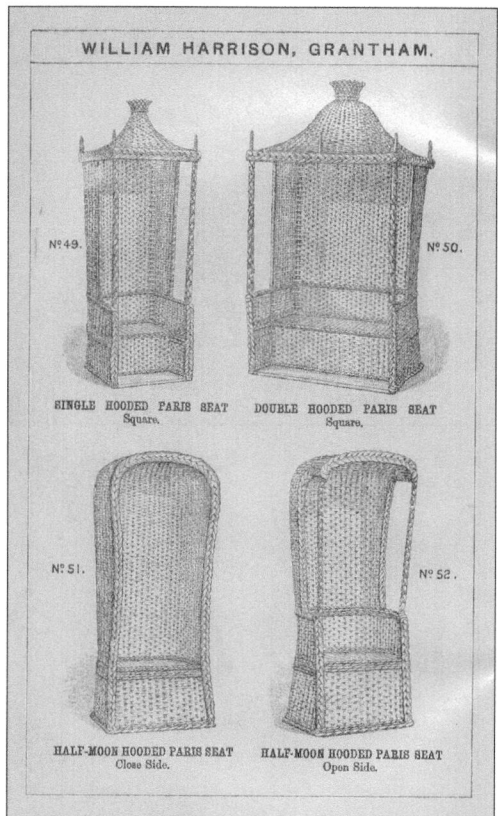

Left: A page from the extensive catalogue showing various hooded seats, priced in the back of the publication from 18s 6d to 58s. In today's decimal coinage this would equate to 92½p for the cheapest seat and £2.90 for the most expensive.

Below: A group of Harrison's workers bundling reeds at the firm's Dysart Road premises in the 1890s. The area was situated close to Westbourne Place.

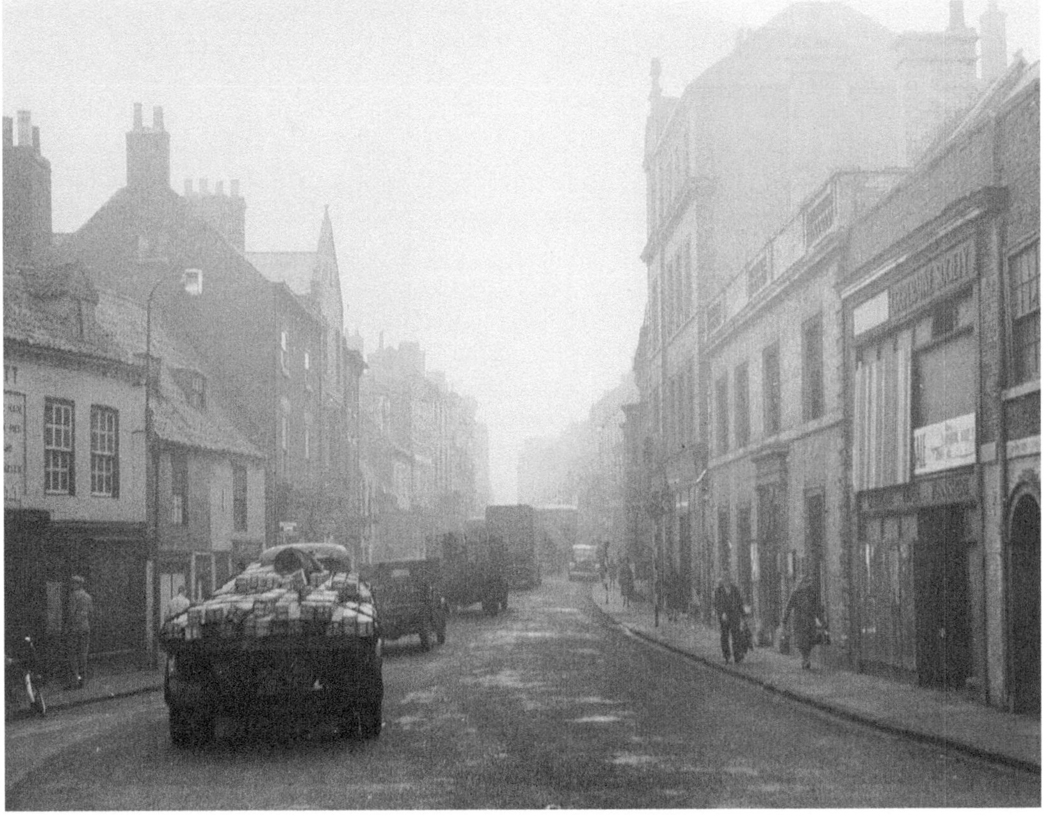

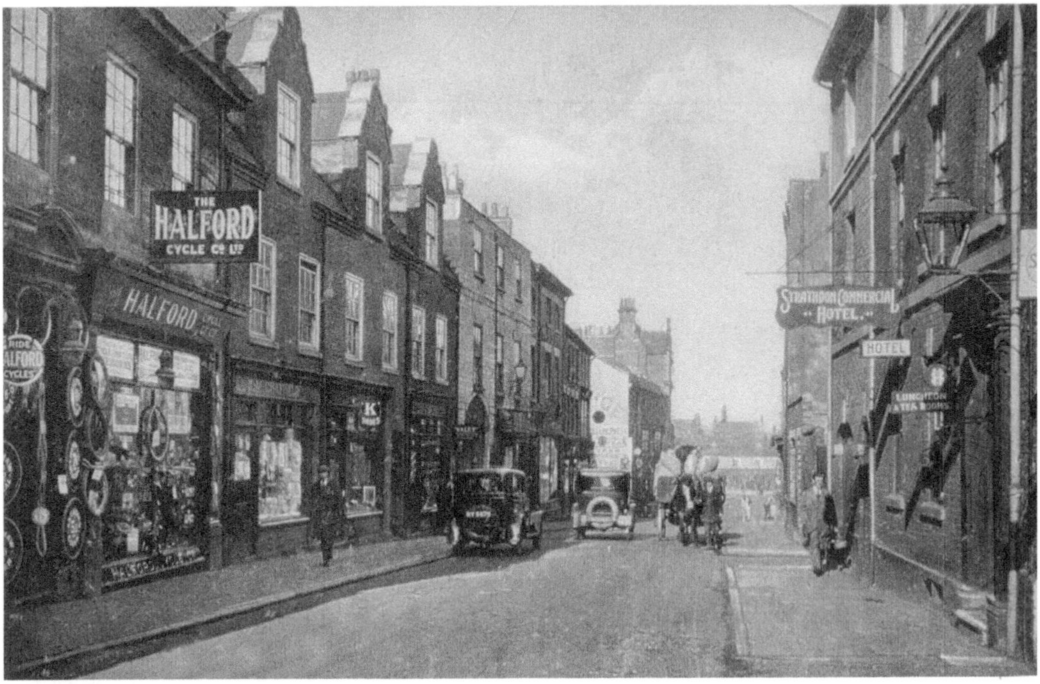
THE
HALFORD
CYCLE Co LTD
HALFORD
RIDE
HALFORD
CYCLES
STRATHDON COMMERCIAL
HOTEL.
HOTEL

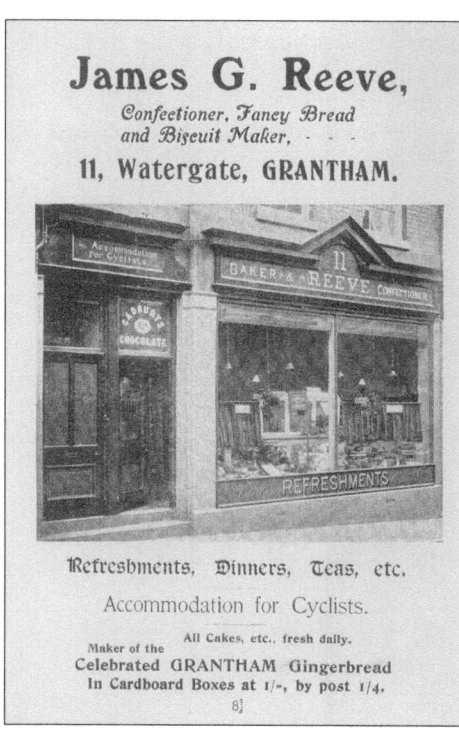

Left: In 1906 No. 11 Watergate was the home of Reeve's bakers and confectioners. They occupied the premises from the late 1890s until just before the First World War. Although the frontage has changed over the years and the shop is now No. 37 Watergate. It has remained a baker's shop for more than a century, a rare island of stability in a changing world of commerce.

Below: This was the top of Watergate in the mid-1940s, little wonder that it was felt necessary to widen the road. Unfortunately it meant the demise of some of the town's oldest buildings. Sharpley's drapers store was one of the first casualties. The building was originally a seventeenth-century town house before becoming a shop in the 1800s.

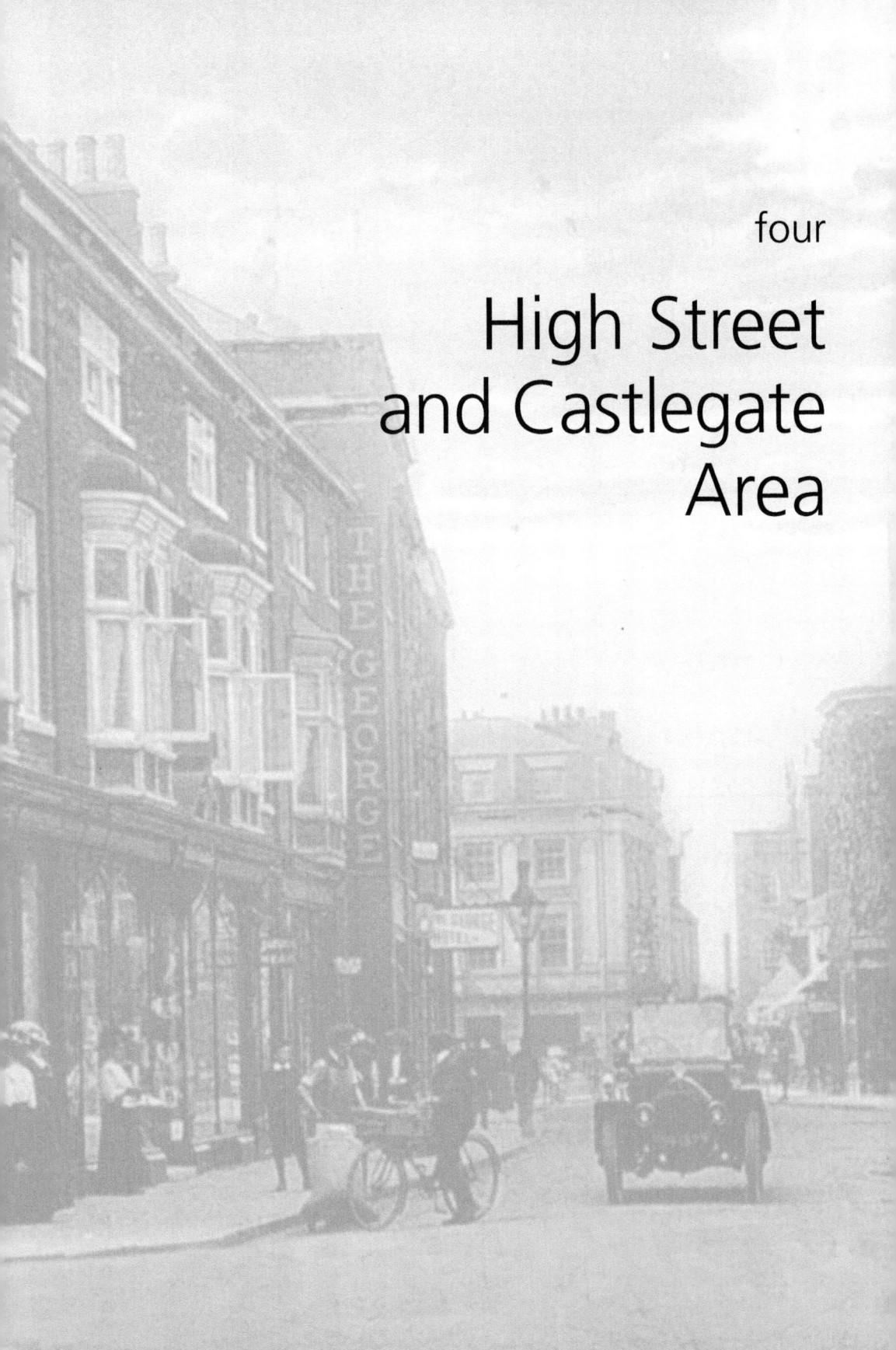

four

High Street and Castlegate Area

Postcard publishers of today like to appeal to the nostalgia in us and produce images from the past on modern cards. The Edwardians often did the same and here we have a card produced around 1905 with a scene dating from the early 1880s. In the centre of the view is The Angel and Royal Hotel, one of the oldest inns in the country. Originally called the Angel Inn it added the royal after the Prince of Wales (later to become Edward VII) came to stay in 1866. On the left of the view can be seen the Noah's Ark, complete with the trade sign of an actual ark above the central doorway. Edward Dickinson ran this general store from the middle of the 1800s until its closure in 1891. The shop was bought by the owners of the hotel next door and incorporated into their premises. On the right of the scene is the old Tudor house that once belonged to the wealthy Seckers family. Soon after this photograph was taken it became a boot and shoe shop before being demolished in 1897. Boots the Chemist moved from the market place and had their own purpose-built shop on the site in the early 1900s.

Almost the same view some forty or so years later in the 1920s. What was once the Noah's Ark is now part of the Angel and Royal Hotel. The spot where the old house of the Seckers had stood is now occupied by Boots the Chemist's rather imposing façade.

The window of the hotel's bar looks down into the Market Place, c. 1930. What sights it must have been witness to over its 800-year history.

Left: A crowd of Granthamians pose for local photographer Walter Wheeler outside the Angel and Royal Hotel amidst the decorations for the coronation of King George V in 1911.

Below: A view of the north end of the High Street on a postcard from the first decade of the 1900s. Sharpley's drapers shop can be seen at the top of Watergate. On the left at No. 71 the chemist's shop of John Newcome stands on the corner of the Market Place. This building was replaced in the 1930s by purpose-built premises for tailors Montague Burton. On the extreme left at No. 70 can be seen the business of Tryner Lynn, outfitter and tailor.

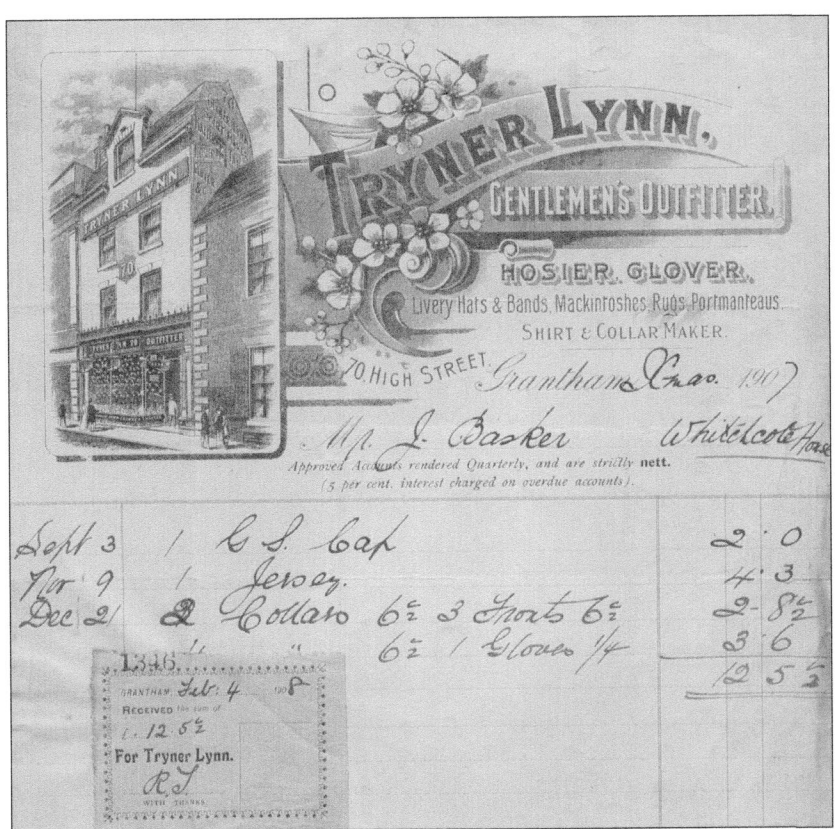

Above: A bill head of Tryner Lynn's dating from 1907. Note the penchant for businesses at this time to exaggerate the size of their premises on this sort of stationary: as can be seen, the people shown in the street are far out of proportion to the shop frontage.

Right: A cabinet photograph of Tryner Lynn, produced in the late 1890s by local photographer Henry Bliss of No. 1 London Road. Not only concerned with his own business he was also involved in the running of the town, becoming mayor in 1901.

Above: Most of this part of High Street disappeared in the early 1930s to make way for the new Marks & Spencer store. The building in the centre of the view had been occupied by the Midland Bank from the early 1900s but for many years before that it had been the chemist's shop of Briggs & Gamble. A view of this can be seen in *Around Grantham*.

Left: Another High Street chemist's shop was William Whysall & Son, almost opposite the previous scene at No. 64. William issued this advertising postcard in 1910. It was one of twelve, each with a month of the year along the bottom and a pretty lady above. The card even came with a hole at the top to pin it up over one's desk or in one's kitchen, a cunning move to ensure William's shop was always uppermost in the mind when thinking of buying his sort of merchandise.

Although in this view encased in ivy, the old Midland Bank is still recognisable in a scene with bunting decorating the town for the coronation of King George V in 1911.

Another day and another coronation, this time the decorations are out for King George VI in 1937. By now Marks & Spencer are well established and have replaced all the shops up to the Maypole Dairy Co. At the time of writing the dairy company's name can still be seen in mosaic at the entrance to the shop and even the brass door handle relates to their business.

Above: There is evidence that there had been a hostelry on the site of the George Hotel as far back as the 1300s, but this Georgian façade dates from the late eighteenth century. By the time this photograph was taken in the early 1930s the archway where the Great North Road coaches would turn in for the night had been equipped with a revolving glass door and the stables round the back had been converted into garages. The hotel closed its doors for the last time in 1989 and the building is now a shopping precinct.

Left: The local historian of today must keep in mind the necessity to save items from the present to pass on to future enthusiasts in years to come. Although this letter head and business card from the George Hotel are only a few years old there is already a generation in the town that will not remember the premises being used for what it was intended.

Above and below: Two rather elegant interior views of the hotel, a welcoming sight to weary travellers who had perhaps spent the day on the dusty roads or just arrived from the railway station in the hotel's own transport.

Almost opposite the George Hotel at No. 20 High Street, on the corner of Finkin Street, the business of printing had been ongoing for nearly 100 years. By 1895 William Clarke had taken over the business of Lawrence Ridge and he was still using up Lawrence's stationary. As can be seen on this bill-head Ridge's name is still over the shop door in the illustration and William is still advertising Ridge's school timetable. Charles Basker was mayor in 1895 and it would appear he was favouring Clarke with his business. No doubt the invitation cards and envelopes were to be sent to a select band of local notables for some grand occasion.

A good selection of types of transport in this view from around 1910. The fine row of shops on the corner of Guildhall Street, called Waterloo House, were demolished in the 1980s. Note the old name for Guildhall Street (Blue Lane) still exists on the wall beneath its more modern title.

Two more of the High Street's hotels can be seen in this 1950s view, the White Hart on the left and the Red Lion on the right. Both sadly are now part of the town's history, the Red Lion closing in the early 1960s and the White Hart in the mid-1980s.

The population has turned out in force to watch the Mayday parade of 1906 pass along the High Street after it had assembled in the Market Place before proceeding to the football ground on London Road where judging of floats was to take place. The old house on the corner of Birdcage Walk was replaced by the Lloyds Bank building in 1921: although Lloyds have since vacated the premises, at the time of writing the building is still used as a bank.

Above: Local bookseller and printer Samuel Ridge published this etching of the parish church in the mid-1800s; it is one of several depicting prestigious buildings in and around the town. As the medieval church of Saint Wulfram owes much to the rich wool merchants of the area, it is perhaps fitting the church's graveyard in this illustration is seen as somewhere 'that sheep may safely graze'. Note the old Georgian façade of No. 1 Church Street to the right of the place of worship.

Left: The majestic spire of the church rises above this scene in Castlegate, *c.* 1905. The building beyond the trees on the corner of Finkin Street is one of the towns' oldest remaining school buildings. The Brownlow Infants School was founded in 1835 to accommodate 130 children.

Above: This cabinet photograph by Frederick George Simpson & Co. of Wharf Road shows group six of the Brownlow Infants School in 1894. Only the style of dress in school photographs change over the years, the facial expressions remain the same. The building ceased to be a school many years ago and the building is now used as offices.

Right: A postcard commemorating the building of Grantham's memorial to Queen Victoria in Castlegate. The premises were built in the first decade of the 1900s and its original use was as a nurses' home. Although today it has lost its look of isolation with more modern structures close by, it still retains the elegant looks seen here 100 years ago.

GRANTHAM ELECTRICITY WORKS,
Exterior and Interior.
Telephone No. 23.
DOLBY BROTHERS, STAMFORD.

Left: Grantham's first electricity works were situated in East Street on the corner of Agnes Street. This advertising postcard shows both an internal and external view of the building. When opened in May 1903 power was limited to the main areas of the town and then only from dusk till 11 p.m.

Below: Another internal view of the building, this time showing the Top Battery Room. When the works opened it must have been something of a wake-up call to the local gas company, who launched an advertising campaign of their own to combat what was at the time a ground-breaking means of providing power.

Top Battery Room.

Grantham Electricity Works.

Electricity Works—

Wharf Road,
Stamford.
Telephone 0306.

East Street,
Grantham.
Telephone 33.

five

St Peter's Hill Area

Above: The Picture House opened on St Peter's Hill during the First World War in 1916. It continued to entertain the town's cinemagoers for forty years before screening its last film in 1956. The bus on the left in this 1929 scene is about to leave the town centre for Great Gonerby and Foston.

Left: An advertising postcard proving that a cinema was once more than just 'somewhere to go to watch a film' — many of these establishments included restaurants, lounges and as shown here, facilities to groom both ladies and gentlemen alike.

Opposite below: The name on the cart is St Vincent's Harrowby Farm and it looks as though these three sturdy horses will need all their strength to get their load back home. Before they do so the photographer captures this moment in time around 1910 using the town's Guildhall as a backdrop.

Above: Just past Blackwell's butchers shop at No. 29 St Peters Hill, a lady looks out from the premises of Joseph Large's hair cutting and shaving rooms. In today's do-it-yourself culture it is easy to forget the age of the cut-throat razor wielded skillfully (we hope) by the man in the barber shop. In this view from the early days of the twentieth century we again see trees standing undisturbed in the road.

A scene captured soon after the Second World War. The other cinema on St Peter's Hill can be seen just beyond the gentleman on the bicycle. The State opened its doors in 1937 and was taken over by the Granada Group in 1960: it was demolished in 1988 to make way for part of the Morrisons' complex.

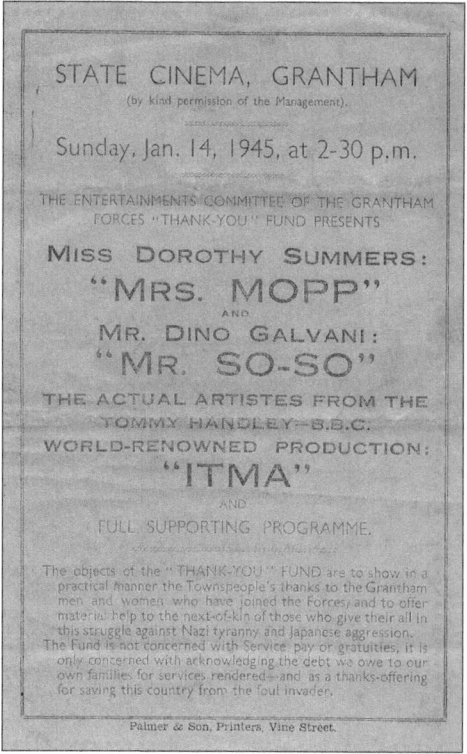

Left: Entertainment included far more than the latest films. From Gracie Fields to Tommy Steele the country's top acts in show business appeared on its stage. This programme from 1945 was for a Sunday afternoon soirée put on by the committee of the Grantham Forces 'Thank-you Fund'. Artists included personalities from the popular BBC 'ITMA' production. The initials stood for 'It's That Man Again', the star of which was Tommy Handley. Although he didn't come on this occasion, another well-known member of the cast, Miss Dorothy Summers (Mrs Mopp), came to amuse the population. Her famous catch phrase was 'Can I do you now sir'.

Opposite below: A group of post office motor drivers and supervising officers pose for the camera in 1935, many proudly wearing medals won in less peaceful times. From left to right, back row: H.E. Willey, F. Hullot, J.E. Horton, J.G. Richardson, F.W. Leachman, M. Mayes, A.E. Neale, F. Bullock. Middle row: A.E. Hallam, F. Hollingworth, W.H. Robinson, M. Cheater, W.H. Marvin, H. Bloodworth, W.L. Loosemore, A. Harrison, W.V. Rowbottom. Front Row: R.B. Taylor, P.R. Grant, G. Greaves (head postmaster), T.A. Lewington, C.A. Naylor.

Above: A view from the extreme south end of St Peter's Hill on a somewhat wet day in 1924. The post office building on the left of the photograph had only been open for two years, the post office having moved from the market place in 1922. It was to serve the town for nearly fifty years before being replaced by the present building in the late 1960s.

The children have turned out in force for this postcard taken around 1910 of St Catherine's Road by prolific national publishers W.H. Smith in their Kingsway series. The Co-operative Society building on the left has long ago lost its wall and railings — sacrificing the iron for the war effort and the brickwork for the need for a wider pavement.

St. Catherine's Road, Grantham.

Grantham Co-operative Society was established in the early 1870s - these premises were built on the corner of St Peter's Hill and St Catherine's Road in 1884 and this 1907 postcard shows the store in all its glory. The different departments start at the grocer's shop on the far right with the butcher's next door and followed by the milliners, fabrics, curtaining etc. The company had their own bakery, dairy and slaughter house in Inner Street and could also supply the townsfolk with coal if required. The writer can remember as a small boy queuing with his mother at the St Catherine's Road entrance to collect the family's share of the Co-op dividend. Commonly known as the 'divi', it was a welcome addition to the household budget.

Opposite below: Opposite the junction on the left into Welham Street, Augers Terrace is shown on this postcard sent home by a soldier serving in the Machine Gun Corps at Belton Camp during the First World War. The row of town houses built in 1874 are no longer covered in ivy and the solid-looking walls and gate posts were replaced long ago by a more open plan style of frontage.

Although the horse and cart would still be in use for haulage of goods for many years after this photograph was taken just before First World War, it does show that the Co-op was looking ahead to more modern means of transportation. The driver and his passenger were still at the mercy of the elements but at least the bread was kept dry.

Traditionally every Boxing Day the Belvoir hounds have met on St Peter's Hill before riding out into the surrounding countryside in the hope of catching a fox. Always an occasion to draw the crowds this gathering in front of the Co-op building in 1906 was two days earlier than usual on Christmas Eve, the Boxing Day meet taking place at Croxton in Leicestershire.

Above: The late Victorians just loved an excuse for dressing up and fancy dress parades were very popular. This one was probably part of the celebrations for the diamond jubilee of Queen Victoria in 1897. The row of small cottages next to the Guildhall was later to become the temporary home for the town's museum until they were replaced by the present purpose-built premises in 1926. The trade sign over the door on the right states that W. Gardener was a horse breaker who also bought and sold the animals.

Right: A view of the Guildhall on a postcard dating from around 1898. These early cards measured 4.5 inches x 3.5 inches as opposed to the later size of 5.5 inches x 3.5 inches. Before 1902 the back was reserved for the address only and a place was left on the front for the message. The Guildhall was designed by William Watkins, a Lincoln man, and built in the late 1860s by William Watnaby. The building replaced the old Guildhall that had stood on the corner of Guildhall Street and the High Street since the 1780s.

For many years the Grantham Fire Brigade headquarters were on the Guildhall premises. This early photograph was taken behind the building and shows the brigade's Newsham manual pump in 1878. It certainly looks as if it was designed to be worked by somewhat younger men than those seen here.

Left: Many of the improvements that took place in the town's fire brigade in the last quarter of the nineteenth century were because of this man's enthusiasm and drive. Sidney Gompertz Gamble was appointed borough surveyor and chief officer of the fire brigade in 1875. He remained in the town for seventeen years until being appointed deputy chief officer of the London Fire Brigade in 1892.

Opposite below: The caption on the postcard states 'testing the new Fire Engine'. On the back of the card is written: 'On the banks of the River Witham, Sept. 26 1907'. To the satisfaction of boater and bowler-hatted gentleman, the delight of several young boys and the consternation of one or two dogs, the fire engine roars into life.

In 1907 the town's new Merryweather steam fire engine poses for the photographer at the back of the Guildhall. This remained the site of the fire station until it moved to its present position on Harlaxton Road in 1946.

Postcards of coronations and other celebratory occasions are reasonably common but scenes of more solemn happenings are a little harder to find. This card shows the Guildhall entrance draped in purple for the day of public mourning when King Edward VII was buried, 20 May 1910.

Opposite below: Three special memorial services were held in town. These were in the Catholic church on North Parade, Finkin Street methodist chapel and the largest at the parish church where the Mayor W. Plumb and the corporation attended. Here they are seen in procession passing shops in the High Street, all closed for the day in respect for the dead sovereign.

Above: Another view of the procession. The Boys' Brigade drummers lead the Boy Scouts and other Brigade members on their journey to the parish church. The base drum is silenced with a covering of mourning purple. Even the public houses closed from noon till 3 p.m., a clear indication of the admiration felt for the late king.

Right: 2,000 of these special booklets were printed and one placed on each seat in the church, the rest were handed out to the many mourners standing in the aisles.

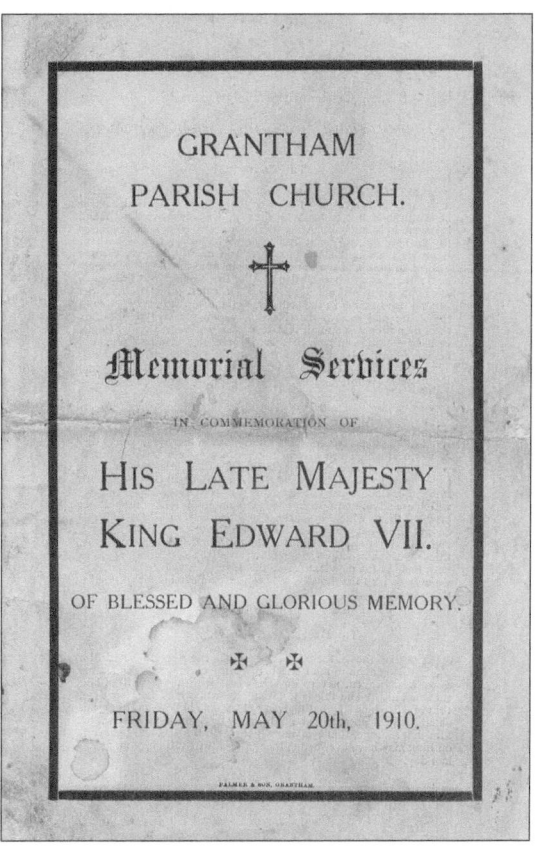

As part of the festivities to mark the coronation of King George VI in May 1937, the mayor, Cllr Arthur Eatch, plants a *Gingko Biloba* tree on the St Peter's Hill Green.

Lawrence Ridge produced this etching of Sir Isaac Newton's statue soon after taking over his father's printing business on the High Street in the early 1860s. The statue, by William Theed, was inaugurated in October 1858, some ten years before the Guildhall was built facing the great man's back. To the left of the statue stands Cheney House at the top of Castlegate. The building was demolished in 1867 and the foundation stone of the new congregational church was laid on the site on the 28 October 1869.

Above: A view of the congregational church dated 1913. The building's official opening took place on 13 October 1870.

Right: A card issued to welcome the Revd W.G. Summers as minister of the church in November 1913. During the First World War he showed understanding and consideration for the troops who were training at the nearby army camps. In 1915 he was appointed officiating clergyman to the soldiers at Belton Camp. In 1922 he resigned his position at the church to become the town's borough librarian.

Above and below: These two postcards of Avenue Road span almost a quarter of a century but it seems little change has occurred in that time. The trees still shade the elegant town houses behind and the age of the motor car is still to reach the stage where it dominates our thoroughfares. The above postcard was sent in 1905 and the one below looking up towards the town centre was posted in 1929.

Above: The 4th Battalion Lincolnshire Regiment (Militia), formerly The Royal South Lincolnshire Regiment (Militia), leaves the Barracks on Sandon Road for the last time on 28 March 1908. The regiment was disbanded, together with several other militia regiments, when the government created the Territorial Army that same year.

Below: The militia marched down St Catherine's Road to St Peter's Hill, along the High Street and down Vine Street to the parish church where, with much pomp and ceremony, their colours were left in the care of the vicar and churchwardens.

The military had not finished with the barracks by any means. In the First World War the building became a military hospital and this view, taken in 1916, shows a group of local civilians about to take soldiers recovering from their wounds for a day out in Stamford on their motorbikes and side-cars. The occasion, arranged by the British Red Cross, was what was known as 'a happy thoughts day'. Makes of motorbike include Royal Enfield, Norton and even an American Harley Davidson.

This fine body of men belongs to the Grantham Voluntary Aid Detachment of the British Red Cross Society. The gentleman in uniform on the right is Mr J.W. Lee, who was the detachment's commandant. They pose with some of their equipment outside the gates to Harlaxton Manor. The stretcher suspended between two bicycles on the left of the scene may look a bit rough and ready in today's age of technology; however, it must have been a welcome sight to wounded soldiers being met at Grantham Station to be transported to the barracks for treatment.

six

The London Road and New Somerby Area

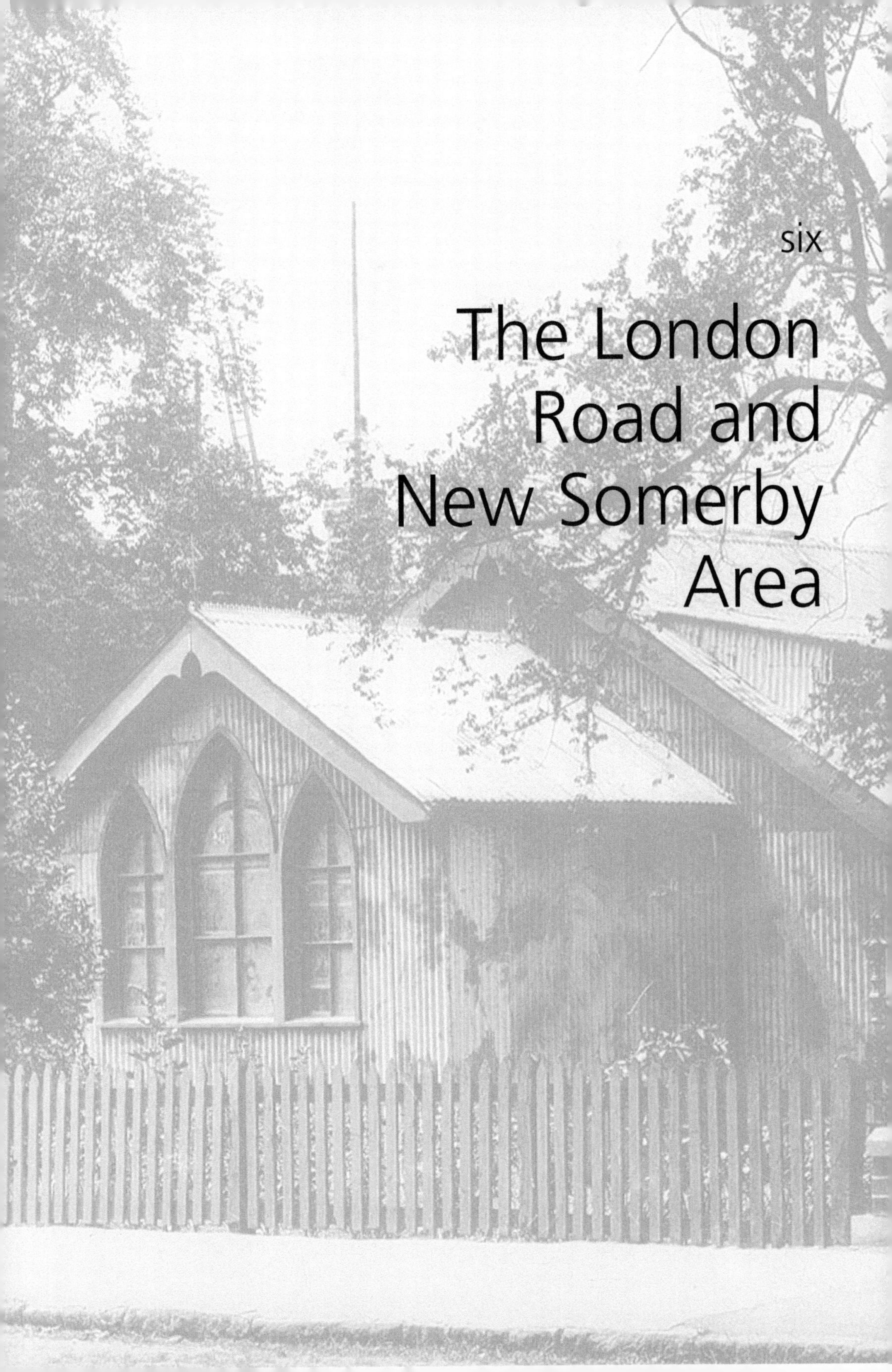

Part of the 1906 May Day Parade makes its way along London Road close to St Peter's Hill. Judging by the way the children are dressed it must have been a particularly cold May Day that year, all appear to be well wrapped in thick overcoats. The second float from the front of the procession has a banner which proclaims it to be the property of Frederick William Skirrey. Fred had a fruit and florist's shop at No. 7 Edward Street. At the time of writing the shops on the right of the scene have only recently been replaced by a block of flats. When this postcard was published the occupants included a branch of Boots the Chemist, Henry Cameron, printer and stationer, John Gollin, cycle maker and agent, John Chambers, boot factor and Charles Waterfield, clothier.

Above: Ruben Barnett established his bakers and confectioner's business in Grantham during the 1890s. The above shop was at No. 5 London Road but he also had premises on the corner of Brook Street and Albion Place. This view dates from 1926 and by this time the business has passed to Alfred Barnett.

Right: As can be seen from this local advert from 1901, the shop was much more than just a bakers: it also traded as a café and even provided beds for the weary traveller. Like several other local bakers Ruben also claimed to supply 'Original Grantham Gingerbread'.

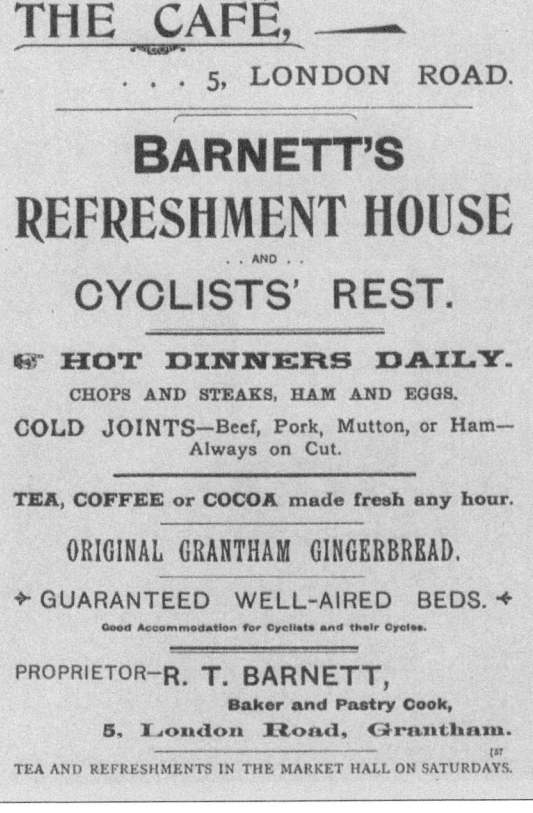

THE CAFÉ,

. . . 5, LONDON ROAD.

BARNETT'S REFRESHMENT HOUSE

.. AND ..

CYCLISTS' REST.

☞ HOT DINNERS DAILY.

CHOPS AND STEAKS, HAM AND EGGS.

COLD JOINTS—Beef, Pork, Mutton, or Ham—Always on Cut.

TEA, COFFEE or COCOA made fresh any hour.

ORIGINAL GRANTHAM GINGERBREAD.

✤ GUARANTEED WELL-AIRED BEDS. ✤

Good Accommodation for Cyclists and their Cycles.

PROPRIETOR—R. T. BARNETT,

Baker and Pastry Cook,

5, London Road, Grantham.

TEA AND REFRESHMENTS IN THE MARKET HALL ON SATURDAYS.

A south-facing view of London Road during the First World War, posted in 1918. Ruben Barnett's shop is the first one on the left with its awning protecting his produce from the heat of the sun.

A similar view around 1960. Barnett's shop can be seen behind the island bollards in the middle of the road. After trading for nearly three quarters of a century Ruben's old shop had now become a branch of Boots the Chemist. Next door can be seen one of the town's old snack bars. The Long Bar was a regular haunt for many of the town's younger generation who liked to drink their frothy coffee from glass cups and feed coins into the American-style jukebox.

Right: The Town and County Liberal Club premises were built in 1897 and for the majority of its existence there has been a shop of some sort in its lower frontage. This view is from the late 1930s when it was occupied by Edward Thomas Burbage. Edward's hairdressers and tobacconists had a well-stocked window and also catered for the passer-by who wished to check on his or her weight. For the princely sum of 1d the scales standing outside the shop would inform them of the damage done by that delicious cream bun.

Below: The Grantham Town and County Liberal Club Committee of 1946. The photograph was taken on the club's bowling green on Dysart Road close to the railway bridge. From left to right, back row: R. Pidd, J.W. Padgett, D.G. Cattermole, G.E. Holvey, C.W. Holmes. Middle row: H.S. Bailey, D.B. Overton, R. Dodd, W. Ryder, A. Corner, E. Eatch, J.W. Handley, J.W. Mears, A.J. Grice. Front row: R. Godber, H. Baxter, H. Bailey, W. Clayton, G.W. Wilson, J.B. Walker, H. Jarvis, B. Wing, A. Bond.

Mowbray's Brewery was situated close to the southern entrance to Rycroft Street on the west side of London Road. The company was established in the 1820s and by the time it merged with J.W. Green of Luton in 1952 the business controlled over 200 public houses in the area.

A group of workers from the brewery pose for the camera in the early 1900s. Unfortunately neither the occasion nor the individual's identities are known. The photograph was probably taken in the company's Brewery Hill premises.

In 1935 lads from Spitalgate School go through their routine on the London Road football ground to re-enact the part they played in the town's celebrations for the centenary of its corporation. The original display took place in Wyndham Park with all the other schools in the town taking part.

After the display it's time for a group photograph, not all the names are known but some can be recorded for posterity. Boys in attendance included: John Burton, Len Stafford, Cyril Pask, Dave Healey, Boris Bennett, Maurice Smith, Chick Chambers, Gomer Dixon, Kenny Rider and Jim Beck. Teachers included the headmaster, Mr A. Aveling and a man that was just as much at home on the sports field as in the class room, Mr C.J.R. Smith.

George Andrew Oldham established his business on the corner of London Road and Inner Street in the 1860s. This view dates from the 1890s and shows George standing in his shop doorway with his son, George Andrew junior. The Oldhams were joiners, cabinet makers and undertakers and helped to keep the town's population supplied with anything from picture frames to coffins. The family name continued trading on this site for approximately 100 years. John Oldham was the last family member to run the business before it was taken over by David Holland as an undertakers in 1969. David's son Robert continued his father's business here until he moved to St Catherine's Road in 2001. Although the old shop premises and the Oldham family name are now long gone, there is still a funeral director's business on the site. The old house seen behind the shop in the above picture was demolished in the first decade of the new millennium.

Opposite below: An early 1950s view of the southern end of London Road. Ralph Mussons sub-post office and grocers occupied No.109 while Cundales chemist's shop was next door. Mason and Cornell's cobblers were adjacent to the Spotted Cow public house and across the vacant lot caused by bombs in the Second World War can be seen the old house built for Richard Hornsby in the early 1800. It was demolished in 1974.

An aerial view of Ruston and Hornsby's works dating from the early 1930s. In the first quarter of the 1800s Richard Hornsby and Richard Seaman moved their blacksmiths business from the village of Barrowby and established their works in Spitalgate at the southern end of London Road. In 1828 Seaman left the business and it remained in the Hornsby family's possession until after the First World War when it merged with Ruston and Proctor Ltd of Lincoln.

Past the junction of London Road, Springfield Road and Bridge End Road the Great North Road continued as South Parade. This tranquil scene was captured on camera in the second decade of the 1900s.

The Grantham Waterworks Co. was formed in 1850 and the works at Saltersford have served the town for well over 100 years. Here workmen from the company are seen replacing the old water main pipes over Spitalgate Bridge in 1906. It must not be forgotten that the main railway line passes beneath this bridge and it is unlikely that the railway company would wish their tight schedules to be disrupted. It would be a daunting task for engineers of today even with all their technology, but in the early years of the 1900s civil engineering works on this scale appeared to be undertaken with little fuss and although perhaps taking longer to complete were mostly done so in a satisfactory manner.

Opposite below: Many of the children living in Albert Street have gathered for their photograph which was put on a postcard and sent to Sheffield in 1908. Although the left-hand side of the street remains much the same today, the houses on the right have all completely disappeared, being replaced by more modern dwellings towards the end of the twentieth century.

The original pumping station at Saltersford was on the east side of the River Witham but by the 1870s this was found to be inadequate for the town's needs. A new Perran Cornish Beam Engine was purchased and was set to work in this purpose-built engine house built on the west side of the river in 1876.

This Blake steam pump was purchased in 1899 to work alongside the beam engine as the need for water increased with the expanding town. There were several other additions in the next few years, including more modern engines run on oil. As a tribute to Victorian engineering it is worth mentioning that the old Cornish Beam Engine was only taken out of service in 1936 after giving stalwart service for sixty years.

Above: Built in the early years of the 1900s Edward Street was originally to be called Howard Street but the name was changed perhaps as a tribute to the reigning monarch, King Edward VII, who came to the throne in 1901. The lady who sent the postcard in 1907 states in the message on the back that 'her new house is marked with a cross'.

Below: Bridge End Road Wesleyan Chapel was built in 1875 but when this postcard was posted in 1905 the assembly rooms and Sunday school on the left of the chapel had only recently been erected. Sadly neither building exists today – the chapel was demolished in the mid-1960s after closing at Christmas 1964. After being home to several nightclubs the assembly rooms lasted until the first decade of the new century before they too were replaced by less imaginative architecture.

Brackenbury's ran this shop on Bridge End Road from before the First World War until the late 1950s. This image dates from the 1920s and according to the message on the back shows Doreen Brackenbury and her nephew Jackie standing in the shop doorway. The business was close to the entrance to Dysart Park gates and must have caught the eye of many a youngster who, after leaving the recreation area, was drawn to the sweets in the window or the home-made ice cream. Father could also buy his daily paper or tobacco and mother could purchase many of her household requirements. These independent corner shops are now mostly part of our country's history, killed off by the supermarkets and our need for one-hit shopping. The premises are still used as a shop today, only now instead of selling bulls' eyes and Fry's chocolate it is a service centre for televisions and videos.

The correct name for this Georgian building is Spitalgate Mill but when the local stationers Needham Brothers produced this postcard in the early 1900s they captioned the image Basker's Mill. The Basker family had run the mill for many years and it was the name most locals used when referring to the premises. In 1918 the mill was bought by Swallow & Sons, another local business with premises at Manthorpe and Barrowby. Since closing as a mill the premises have been used for various purposes but at the time of writing it has been divided up into very attractive dwellings.

This view from the bottom of Somerby Hill dates from 1907 and although it is captioned Somerby Road it is in fact still part of Bridge End Road. The thoroughfare has been widened over the years and there is now housing on the right side of the road.

Much of Dudley Road was built in the last quarter of the nineteenth century. Dudley Terrace, the neat row of dwellings on the right, has a date stone of 1882.

Above: The wall on the left in this view taken around 1900 of Harrowby Road encloses part of Grantham's main cemetery, opened in 1857 after the burial ground on Manthorpe Road was found to be inadequate for the town's needs.

Opposite below: The inside of the church on a postcard sent in 1907. By this time the church had closed, being replaced by the present church on the opposite side of the road close to the cemetery. The first service in the new St Anne's church took place in May 1907.

Above: A postcard of the first St Anne's church on Harrowby Road. It opened in January 1884 to cater for the growing population of New Somerby. The building was fondly nicknamed 'The Tin Tabernacle' by the locals because of its construction from iron sheeting.

Another view of the old church, this time showing the parish room behind. Although the church was demolished 100 years ago the parish room still exists today, sandwiched between houses in Cecil Street and Harrowby Road.

Two ladies talk over the garden gate of one of the homes that were built on the site of the old iron church. Seen on a postcard sent in 1920, the row of houses is located between King Edward Terrace, built in 1902, and Newton Terrace, built in 1904.

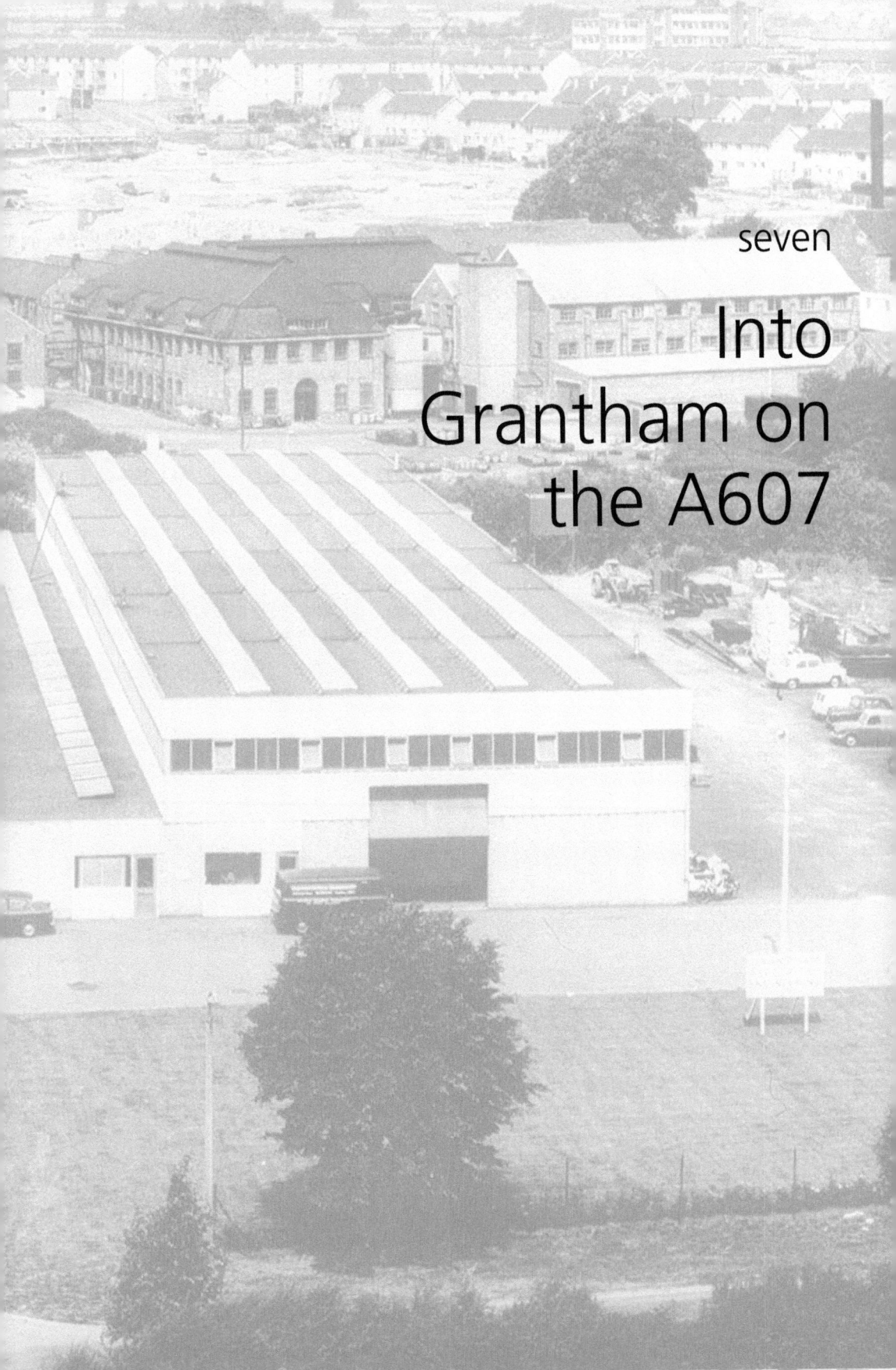

seven

Into Grantham on the A607

In this age of leisure it is easy to forget that the country's canals were mainly built for commercial reasons. When many main roads were nothing more than dusty or muddy tracks these waterways carried the nation's goods throughout the land. The Grantham to Nottingham Canal was opened in the late 1790s and by 1863 Alexander Shaw had opened his parchment works along its banks. In the 1870s he was joined by John Shaw and the company added leather dressers and fellmongers to its description. The premises were situated down Hollis's Lane (now Earlesfield Lane) off Harlaxton Road. The print shows the factory complex sometime around 1900.

By the early 1920s Shaw's had gone bankrupt and the premises were later occupied by Bjorlow Tanneries. The above photograph of some of the workforce outside one of the factory buildings has a note on the back stating the date to be the late 1930s. Unfortunately it does not identify any of the men or the lady in the group.

A view of the tannery looking over the factory of Grantham Electrical Engineering on Harlaxton Road. This early 1970s view shows the leather works just before it closed in 1973. The top of the photograph shows houses being built on the growing Earlesfield Estate.

A similar view some ten years later; Grantham Electrical Engineering now has a new office building and the tannery has disappeared, being replaced by a group of industrial units on what is now called Hollis Road.

Above: One of a series of First World War postcards showing the 11th Northern Division leaving Grantham in 1915. The Division had been training at Belton Park Army Camp. They are here seen on Harlaxton Road on their way to the military railway sidings on Springfield Road to embark on the first stage of their journey to take part in the 'war to end all wars'. In the background just before the houses on the left is the lane that led to the Grantham Gas Works.

A copy of the Grantham Gas Co.'s report of the directors dated 31 December 1898. This year the company paid dividends of ten per cent and the directors appeared confident that the good times would continue for the foreseeable future. Little did they know that by the early 1900s power supplied by electricity would provide a competitive power source that would eat into the company's profits.

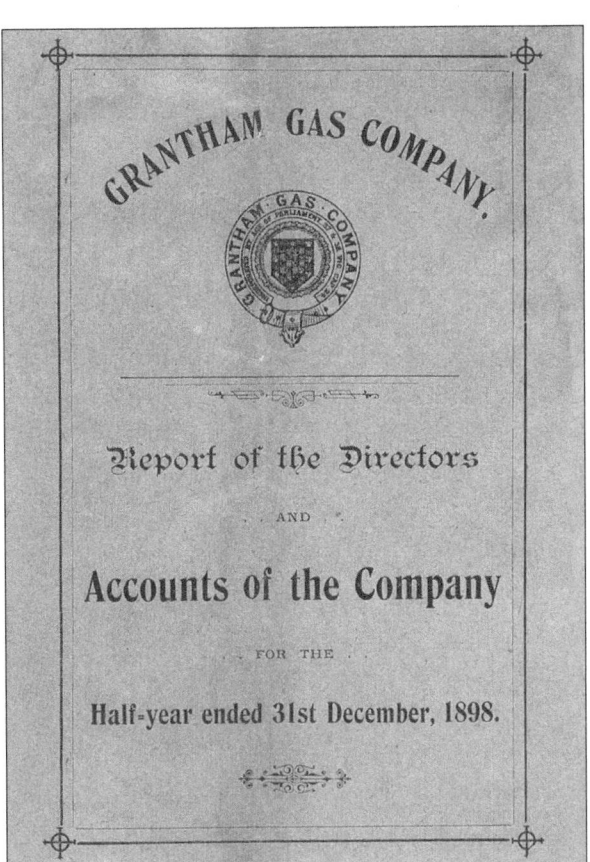

Right: A bill from the Grantham Gas Co. dated September 1883. The amount of gas used by Mr Newcombe of Castlegate from April to July of that year cost him the princely sum of 2s 2d.

Opposite below: A late 1800s view of Grantham Gas Works, situated close to the canal off Harlaxton Road. There had been a gas house on the Earle's Fields since 1833. Originally called Grantham Gas Light & Coke Co. the name changed to simply Grantham Gas Co. in the 1860s. It supplied the town's gas for over 100 years before it ceased production in the late 1950s.

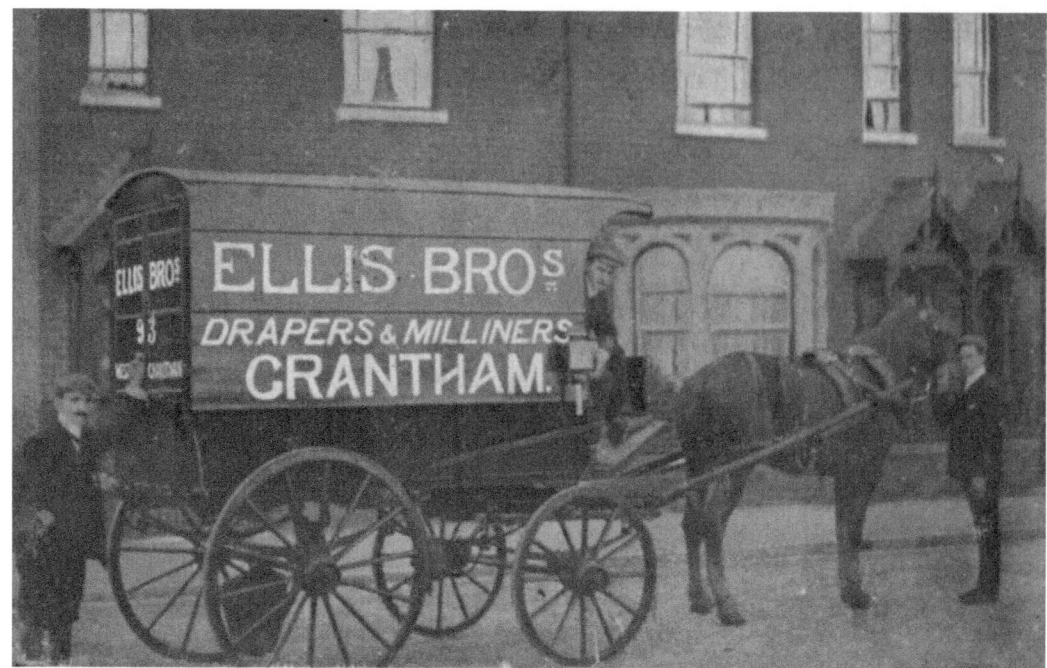

Ellis Brothers' Drapers and Milliners shop was located at No. 93 Westgate, but here we see their delivery cart parked outside what is now No. 146 Harlaxton Road. The block of houses between Gasworks Lane and the south-western entrance to Alexander Road were originally Nos 1-8 Coronation Terrace (later Coronation Villas). Ellis's cart stands outside No. 8 sometime around 1910.

In August 1922 Grantham suffered its worst floods for many years after almost twenty-four hours of torrential rain caused the River Witham and the Mowbeck to burst their banks. The above view shows a water pump in action at premises in the northern entrance to Alexander Road.

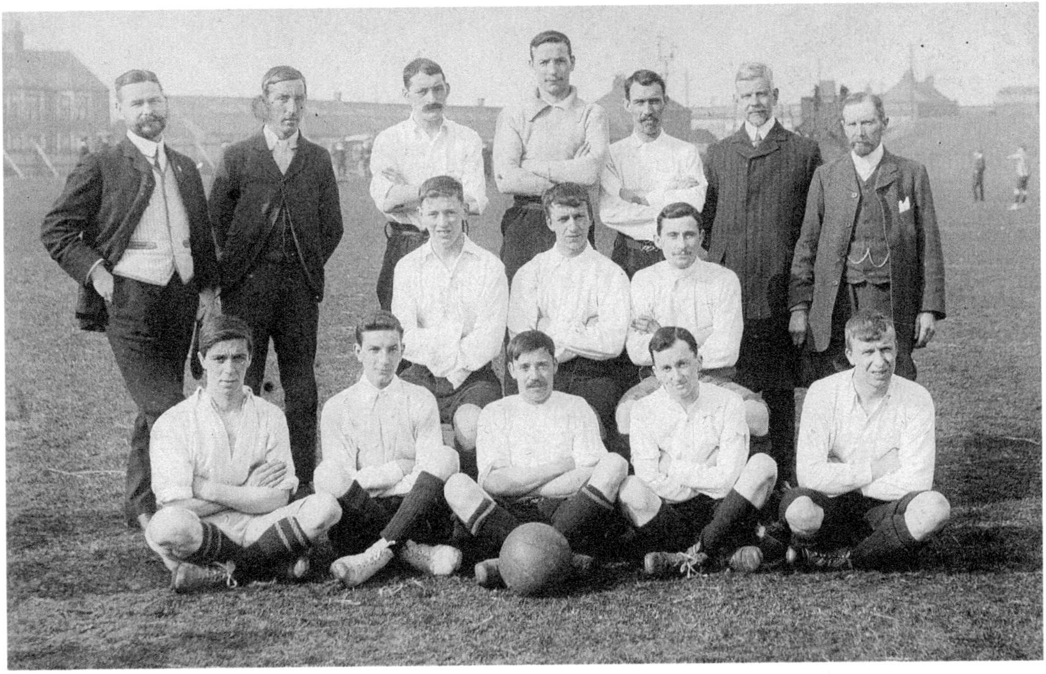

In the first half of the 1900s there was a sports ground on the eastern side of Harlaxton Road close to the railway bridge. Most of it has since been used for housing and commerce but in its heyday the venue was a popular site for recreational activities. The above postcard shows the Bridge End Road Wesleyan chapel's football team posing for their photograph just before kick off, *c.* 1910. From left to right, back row: ?, F. Watchorn, G. Armitage, Basford, Towers, -?-, Bowler. Middle row: Swain, -?-, Pick. Front row: P. Waite, ?, Littledyke, -?-, Swain.

Kindly Bring This Catalogue

CATALOGUE OF THIRD ANNUAL

FOAL SHOW AND SALE

HARLAXTON RD. CRICKET GROUND, GRANTHAM,

On Monday. Sept. 17th. 1906.

FOR ANIMALS INSURED WITH THE COUNTY LIVE STOCK INSURANCE ASSOCIATION LTD. YORK

AND OTHERS

THE SUFFERING OF ANIMALS

THE ELLIMAN FIRST AID BOOK

ELLIMAN'S ROYAL EMBROCATION

THE ELLIMAN FIRST AID BOOK

ELLIMAN, SONS & CO., SLOUGH, END.

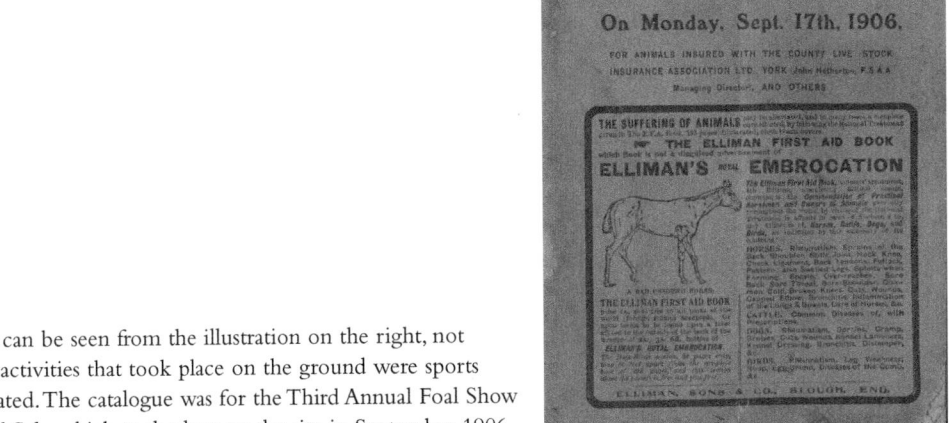

As can be seen from the illustration on the right, not all activities that took place on the ground were sports related. The catalogue was for the Third Annual Foal Show and Sale which took place on the site in September 1906.

The 1906 Grantham rail crash is well documented in other publications but few photographs illustrate the carnage better than the one above. Twelve people were killed at the scene and two died later from their injuries. Amongst the dead were the driver and fireman. The cause of the accident remains a mystery to this day.

Most of the wreckage finished down the embankment just past the railway bridge straddling Harlaxton Road and Old Wharf Road. This postcard by Davage of Newark shows a gang of men working on the damaged parapet of the bridge with onlookers standing in Old Wharf Road.

Above: A view of the west end of Wharf Road in the early 1900s. All the buildings on the left of the view have now been replaced by a supermarket and its car park. The majority of these premises were small town houses where close-knit communities dwelt near to the centre of the town. Just past the three boys on the left is the entrance to Rutland Street, with Stanton Street a few yards further along marked by the sign for The Sir Isaac Newton public house hanging on the corner. On the extreme right of the view was the entrance to what had been Richard John Boyall's carriage works.

Right: An advertisement for Richard Boyall's carriage and harness works appearing in a publication dated 1872. The majority of the premises have long ago disappeared but the square building on the left remains in use to this day. The illustration looks over the premises from Station Road.

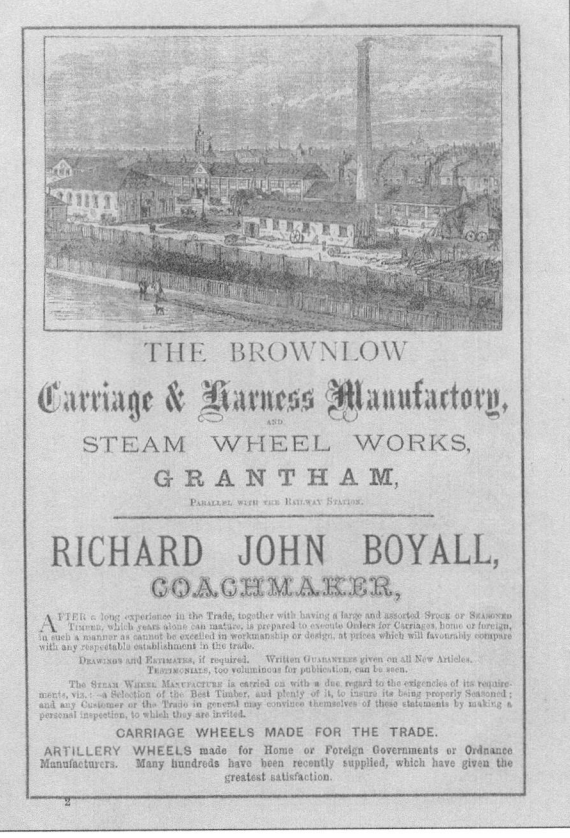

By the turn of the twentieth century B. & J.V. Coultas had taken over most of the site of Boyall's carriage works. Called the Victoria Saw Mills, the business provided the area with English and foreign timber and supplied the agricultural community with poultry houses, field gates, tumbrels, sheep troughs, and shepherds' huts etc. By this time the square building on the left had been used as a drill hall and orderly room for the military, a roller skating rink and during the First World War became the King's Picture House. In 1918 it was used by The Young Men's Christian Association (YMCA). Today at the time of writing it is the home of a builder's merchant.

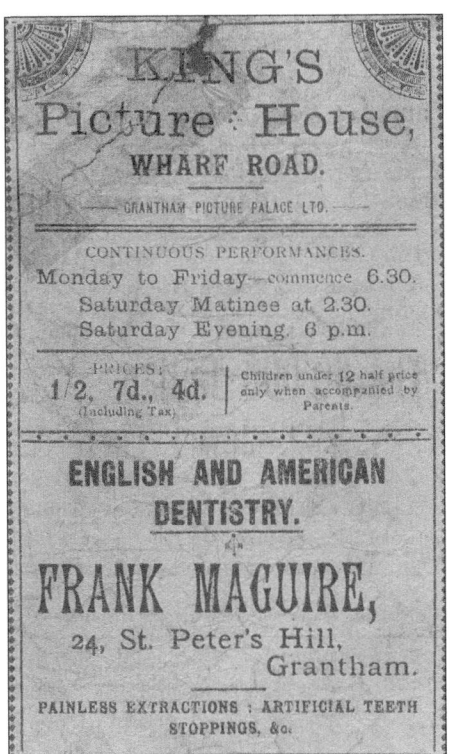

Above left and right: A programme from the King's Picture House listing the delights to be enjoyed for the week commencing 5 April 1917. Prices ranged from 4d to 1s 2d; however, as stated bottom right, if an order for lights out was issued there would be no refund.

Right: Jack Neal at one time worked as projectionist at the King's Picture House but as can be seen from his attire in the photograph, he also enjoyed performing on stage and was an entertainer in his own right.

CROSS OF LEGION OF HONOUR
PURVEYORS OF MUSTARD AND STARCH TO THE KING
THE LARGEST MUSTARD MANUFACTURERS IN THE WORLD

COLMAN'S No1 STARCH
COLMAN'S MUSTARD
COLMAN'S No1 AZURE BLUE
COLMAN'S CORN FLOUR
COLMAN'S SELF RISING FLOUR
ASK FOR COLMANS D.S.F. MUSTARD

11 190

Bought of CHESHIRE & SON,
Wholesale & Retail Cash & Drug Stores,
63, Wharf Road, GRANTHAM.

24 Dozen (assorted) Drinks
or a few
Clarette Ginger ale Lemonade
Orange Champagne, Nectar,
Lime Juice & Soda

& oblige
L. D. Cheshire

Ask for (KEEN) ROBINSON'S WAVERLEY OATS.

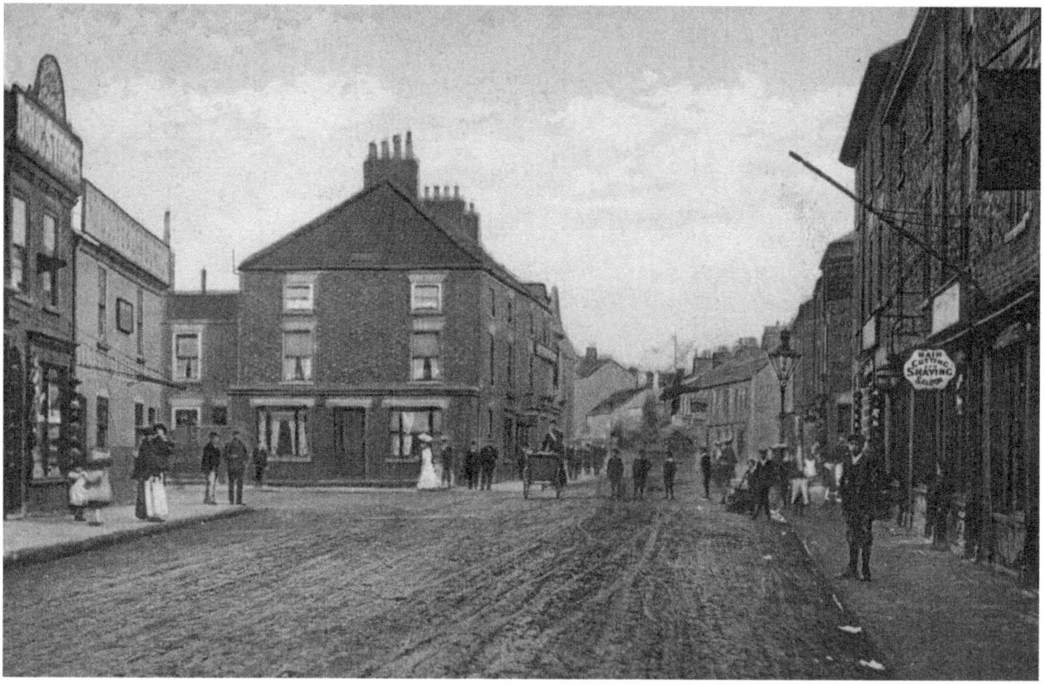

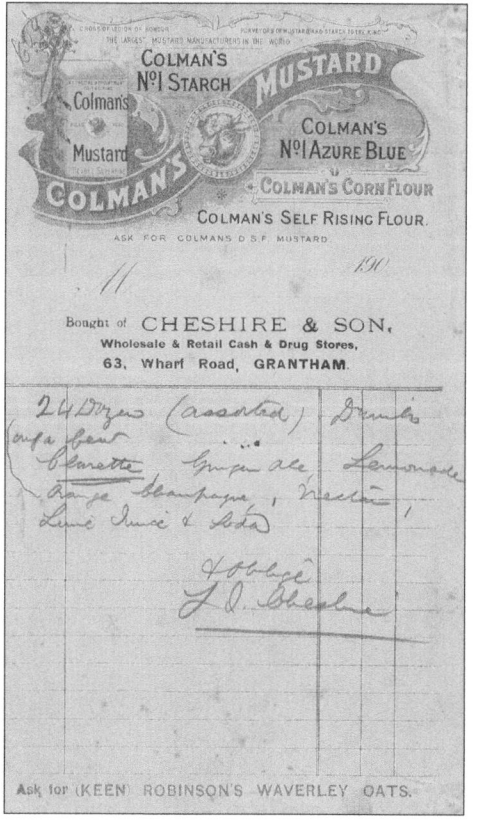

Above: In 1907 Connie Vincent sent this postcard of Wharf Road home to her sister in Hampstead. She states in the message on the back that she has marked their grandad's shop with a cross. The girl's grandfather was Bertram George Skipworth, a chemist whose premises were at No. 15 Wharf Road on the corner of Commercial Road. The premises of Cheshires, another Wharf Road chemist, can be seen on the left of the view.

Left: A billhead from Cheshires, about the same date as the above postcard. Large companies like Colman's would issue this sort of stationary to local businesses who would then stamp their own name in the space provided.

eight

Westgate and the Market Place

When Boots the Chemist issued this postcard around 1910, Wide Westgate was exactly that. The age of the motorcar and on-street parking were many years in the future, allowing the photographer to safely set up his equipment in the road to capture this Edwardian scene for future generations to admire.

A view of Westgate about the same date looking south-west from the end of Guildhall Street. There appears to be an open-air auction in progress (a site used for many years by local sale rooms). Amongst the businesses on display are three of the town's lost public houses. On the right just past Menzies Journalists & Sports Outfitters can be seen the sign for the Shepherd & Dog, while over the road, close to the unattended cart, are the Black Horse and the Fox & Hounds.

An early 1900s photograph showing a view of the Black Horse public house in Westgate when Eliza Linnel was the licensee. Here she is seen standing near the doorway of her premises with others who were probably members of her family. The sender of the card has named them as follows – Fred stands in the doorway on the left with Flossie near the window, next is Lissie (Eliza) with 'the boy Lionel'. The other two young Ladies were Doris and Nellie. The pub closed in 1910 and the premises were taken over by the Fox and Hounds next door. The business to the left of the Black Horse was one of several in the town catering for the growing number of cyclists taking to the roads in Edwardian England. In this scene it was the premises of John William Lee and his wife Sarah, who had recently taken over the shop from George Budd.

A quiet scene in Narrow Westgate, belying the commercial activity that has always existed in this part of Grantham. From long before this 1900s view to the present day, business activity has always been busy and varied. On the extreme right is the Blue Ram public house (this has since reverted back to its original name the Kings Arms). Other businesses on view are butchers, printers, hatters and hosiers. On the corner of a short cut through to the George Hotel yard was one of Grantham's cutlers and gunsmiths, William Stovin. Past Palmer's Bakery can be seen George Willoughby's trade sign of the Little Dustpan. Although George's hardware and fancy goods store has long since ceased trading the sign remains over the shop to this day.

Samuel Ridge issued this engraving of the Westgate Hall soon after the building was erected in 1852. Originally built as one of the town's two corn exchanges (the other being on the High Street) it has been used for many activities over the years. At the time of writing it is home to one of the town's nightclubs.

Above: Although this postcard was posted in 1910 the scene shows the Market Place in the mid-1890s. The obelisk that replaced the market cross in the 1880s was itself replaced when the cross was reinstated in 1911. In the time between George Willough moving his trade sign of the Little Dustpan from his shop in the Market Place to No. 2 Westgate, he spent a short period as licensee of the Royal Oak next to Haines' tailors. George was a man that knew the power of advertising and the Little Dustpan can be seen displayed on the upper bay window of the public house.

Below: The participants of the 1906 May Day Parade assemble in the Market Place before proceeding along the High Street to the London Road sports field.

Above: An 1870s scene in the Market Place issued on a *carte de visit* by the London photographers' firm of Provost & Co. The Old Blue Sheep Inn to the right of the Conduit closed in 1915 with the larger and imposing Blue Lion Inn to the right of the cross holding on until 1969. However, unlike its smaller companion the building still exists today. Now called Lindpet House, it is the home of several company offices. The large building on the right was occupied by John Hall, who at this time was an undertaker, upholsterer and kept in stock several examples of the pianoforte. He also traded china and glassware from the smaller shop next door. In the early 1890s another floor was added to the china shop and it became the general post office. Both Hall's and the post office were to move to St Peter's Hill in the 1920s.

Left: A seasonal postcard advertising the various treasures that could be obtained from John Hall's for Christmas gifts, *c.* 1905. By now the firm was listed in the trade directories as 'complete house furnishers'.

Above and below: Shortly after the local men that had survived the First World War returned home it was decided to give them an official welcome in gratitude for the part they had played in the conflict. At twelve noon on 7 August 1919, the men assembled in the Market Place. To the strains of military marches played by the band of the Machine Gun Corps they moved off in true army fashion, their destination the King's School field on North Parade where a fine meal awaited consisting of cold meats, pickles, fruit tarts, custards, cheeses and a liberal quantity of beer. The two postcards on this page show the men leaving the Market Place as they march past the Home and Colonial Stores and Edward Nickerson's confectionary shop (now the homes of Lloyds Pharmacy and a model shop).

The men turn the corner at the top of the Market Place and turn left into Watergate on their journey to the North Parade Sports Field. The entire route was lined by the local population who had turned out in force to witness the occasion.

On their arrival at the field the men formed up to hear an address by Lord Brownlow, seen here on the left talking to Maj.-Gen. R.O. Kellett. After the meal many took part in a programme of sports consisting of various races and competitions including a sack race, three-legged race, obstacle race, tug of war and a football match played in sacks. There was even an event for one legged ex-soldiers who threw a cricket ball while sitting on a chair.

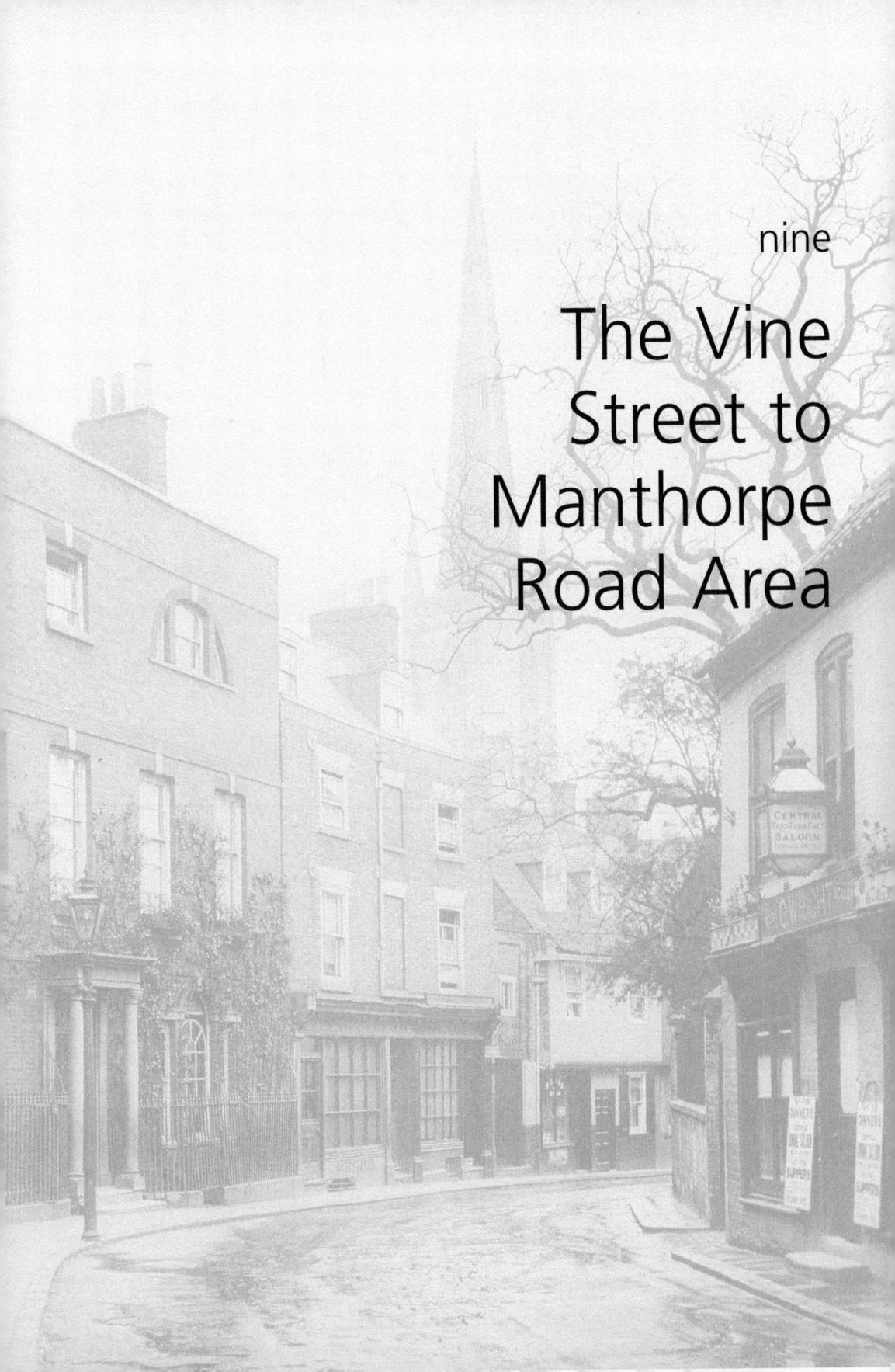

nine

The Vine Street to Manthorpe Road Area

An unknown photographer has ventured out on a wet day towards the end of the first decade of the 1900s to record this view of Vine Street with the spire of the parish church looking down on the proceedings. In the early 1700s Vine Street was little more than a pedestrian route from the church to the High Street but over the years it gradually developed into a street containing its own business community and a roadway capable of taking traffic. On the left is the elegant façade of Vine House, a Georgian dwelling built in the 1760s. Next door at No. 6 was the premises of Herbert Bell, upholsterer and undertaker. By the 1920s his shop was taken over by William Read, dyer and cleaner, who was already at No. 7. Next to Reads at No. 8 was the home of Thomas Turner, baker and confectioner. Across the road on the extreme right is the well-advertised premises of the Central Fish and Chip Saloon run by Charles Wright.

Swinegate bedecked with decorations for the coronation celebrations of Edward VII in 1902. The photograph was reproduced on a postcard by George Scothern in 1935 when the town was again festooned with bunting, this time for the Silver Jubilee of George V.

A postcard of the bottom of Swinegate looking south, c. 1905. The mother on the left standing outside the shop of Edward Sivers proudly holds up her baby to make sure the photographer captures her child's likeness for future generations to admire. Part of the block of tall buildings on the right have now made way for the exit from the Watergate car park.

Left: On the left of this quiet 1901 view of Brownlow Street is one of Grantham's oldest buildings, erected in the 1650s for Thomas Hurst in what was then Little Gonerby. Through the trees on the corner of Brook Street and Swinegate, adorned with advertising posters, is what had been Grantham's old theatre. Demolished in the early 1950s the building lost its thespian connections many years ago and had since been used by a variety of businesses; when this photograph was taken it was being used as a warehouse for a local corn merchant.

Below: When Walter Wheeler published this postcard in the early years of the 1900s the geography of his caption was slightly amiss – the scene is actually in Brook Street with Dawson's almshouses on the left of the view. Built in the 1860s the ten dwellings are named after George Dawson who generously left money and property which is used for their upkeep.

Above: A postcard of Redcross Street sent to Boston in October 1909. Several of the houses have date stones from the 1880s but this is one of the few Grantham streets that has seen little structural change over the years.

Below: Greenlawns, situated behind houses on the south side of Redcross Street, is now used as a school sports field, but when this image was captured on camera in the early 1900s it had a fine croquet lawn and tennis courts. Although the circular seat has long ago disappeared the pavilion still stands as a reminder of those long hot Edwardian summers often depicted in period films and novels.

Above: The name of Alford Street used to be River Street. It was changed to its present name in the late 1800s perhaps in honour of Lady Alford, the mother of the then 3rd Earl Brownlow. The trees at the bottom of the road have now made way for a modern housing development.

Grantham streets and thoroughfares were bedecked with decorations in 1935. Not only was it the Silver Jubilee year of the sovereign but the town also celebrated 100 years since the creation of its corporation. Here local photographer George Scothern has captured a scene in Manthorpe Road. The old stone-built house sporting the flags was once The Seven Stars Inn. Dating from the early seventeenth century it closed as a public house in the mid-1800s and has been a private dwelling ever since.

Above: Taken from the parish church in July 1905, this photograph looks over the gardens of Grantham House on the right with the backs of houses in Redcross Street on the left. The view captures the impressive display of sheds and parade grounds established for the 1905 Lincolnshire Agricultural Show. The show was held on ground which, in 1924, was to become part of Wyndham Park, established as the town's memorial to its menfolk lost in the First World War.

Opposite below: A group of ladies pose on their float outside Exeter House in Park Road. Dressed as gypsy peg sellers, they are probably about to take their place in the procession as part of the festivities to celebrate the Silver Jubilee of King George V in 1935.

Oh Halcyon days! Long before this part of Grantham became Wyndham Park the area had been a popular place where the townsfolk congregated to enjoy the great outdoors. Known as The Recreation Field it was a place where young and old alike could relax and enjoy the simple pleasures of life. Captured by the camera of an unknown photographer, the scene shows local children making the most of a fine summer's day sometime around 1905. Just over the youngsters' heads, middle right, can be seen what was then the new Belton Lane Bridge over the River Witham, the cast-iron structure replaced the old ancient stone bridge in the late 1890s.

ten

Out on the A607

Above: Manthorpe High Road on a postcard used in 1912. The houses on the extreme left have a date stone of 1849. The church of St John the Evangelist, whose spire can be seen in the middle of the view, was built in the same decade. About a mile out of Grantham on the A607 the village has now almost been engulfed by Grantham's urban sprawl.

Below: A similar view shortly after the First World War. By now the road has been widened, curbed and metalled with a footpath created on the right of the scene.

Right: Mabel sent this card to her friend Lettie in 1915. It shows a view of Manthorpe Low Road close to the turning that now leads to the village hall and the banks of the River Witham. Mabel tells her friend that they have just killed a pig and are now busy rendering lard. She has put crosses on the card showing the location of both her bedroom and sitting room.

Below: Another scene in Low Road, this time dating from the 1920s. The view is from the northern end of the road looking towards Grantham.

During the First World War, Belton Park was the home to a large army camp. To keep it supplied the authorities built a railway which joined the main line to the west and crossed the A607 close to the T-junction with the lane, which at that time joined the highway to the Great North Road just outside the village of Great Gonerby. This photograph was taken by the Belton photographic studios of T.H. Burnett. The group consists of soldiers serving at the camp – two engineers, manual workers and a small lad dressed in army uniform. The two engineers, front row seated, third and fourth from the right are wearing badges of the Royal Engineers in their left lapels, perhaps to deter overzealous young ladies eager to present white feathers to young men out of uniform. The occasion is not known but it was popular at the time to dress young lads in uniform for recruitment rallies, official ceremonies or other patriotic functions.

Opposite above: The 89th Brigade were part of the 11th Northern Division who were training at the camp in the early years of the war. The Brigade was nicknamed the Liverpool Pals. The Pals Brigades were so-called because of the way whole communities joined up and were kept together, a system later abandoned because of the losses sustained in battle to localities back home. This souvenir multi-view card of the camp was sent home to Liverpool by Willie Shepherd. The message on the back is to his father and Willie tells him about the camp, what the weather is like and a recent inspection by Murray, 'Kitchener's right hand man'.

Opposite below: Soldiers of the 89th Brigade gather for a drumhead sermon in Belton Park with the huts of the camp spread out behind.

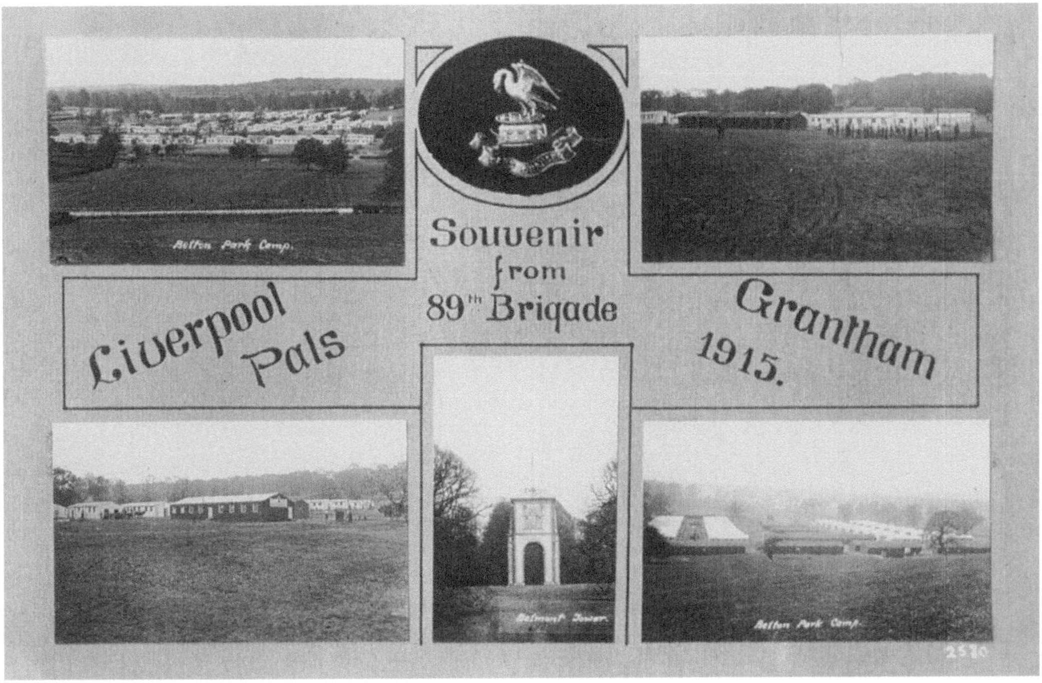
Belton Park Camp.
Souvenir from 89th Brigade
Liverpool Pals
Grantham 1915.
Belmont Tower.
Belton Park Camp.
2580

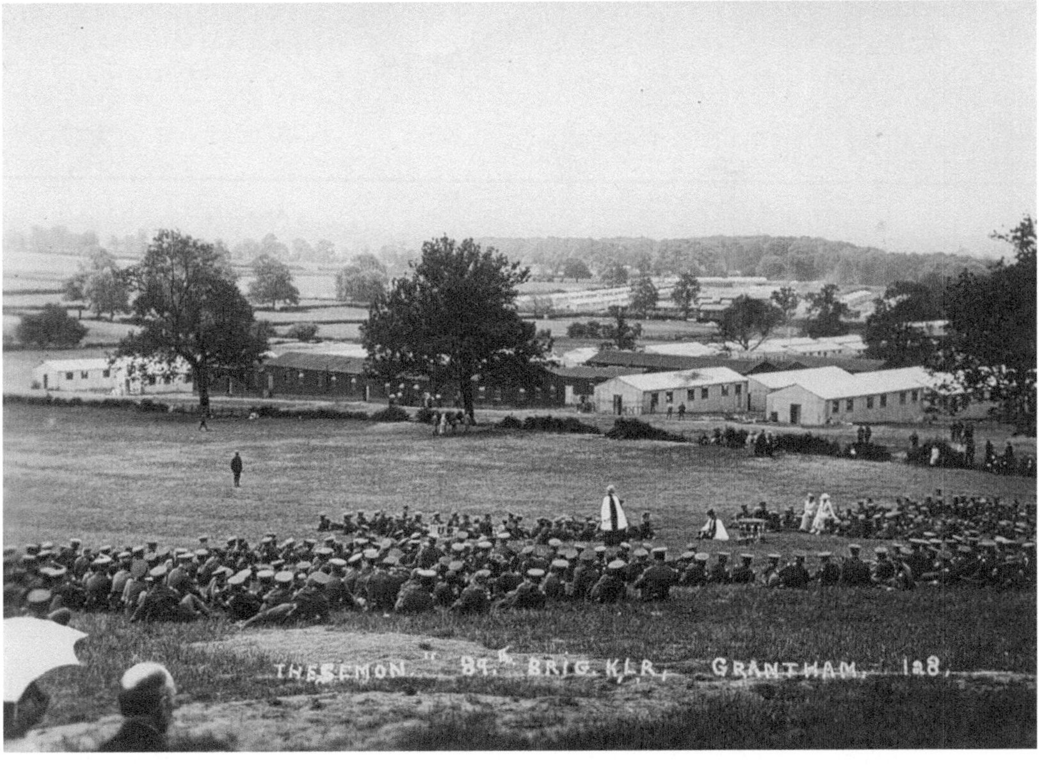
THE SERMON. 89th BRIG. K.L.R. GRANTHAM. 128.

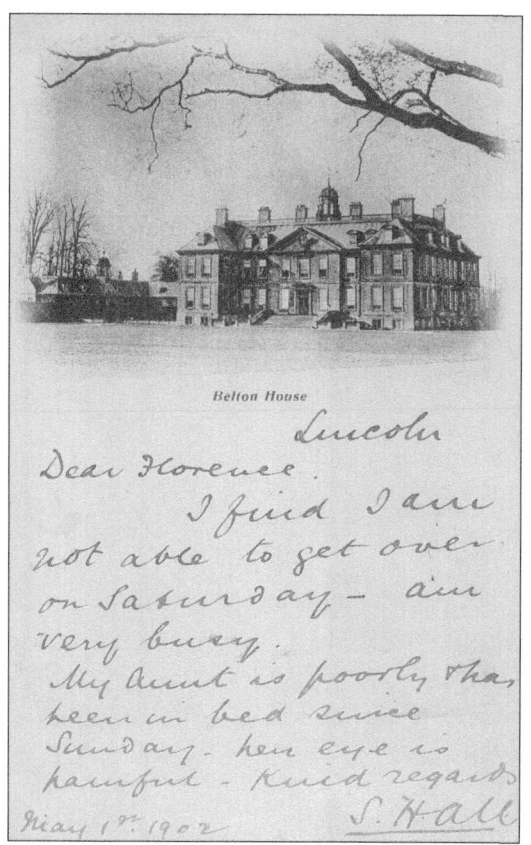

Left: The seventeenth-century Belton House on a postcard from before the end of 1902. The back of the card was reserved for the address only and all messages had to be written on the space left below the picture on the front. The house was designed by William Winde and built in the 1680s for Sir John Brownlow. Now run by the National Trust the property is a popular venue for visitors, either soaking up the history and treasures of the house or enjoying the gardens and grounds outside.

Below: Belton Village, two and a half miles north-north-east of Grantham, is now bypassed by the A607, but when this postcard was sent in 1916 the main road still passed through the village. Soldiers from the nearby army camp stand in the road close to the old school.

Above: A clearer view of the village school published by local Grantham man Walter Wheeler. Although the building still exists today the children have long gone from its classroom, together with the old school bell that once summoned them to their lessons.

Below: Today these seventeenth-century Bede Houses are two private residences but in 1913, at the time of this photograph, it was still a home to these elderly village ladies. The gable end on the left has the original date of 1659 and the one on the right a date of 1827 when further work was carried out on the premises.

A postcard produced by Grantham stationers Needham Brothers in the second decade of the 1900s when the village pump was still in use. The old pump also served as a milestone, stating on its pillar that the journey to London is 112 miles and a trip to Lincoln twenty-three miles.

Built in the 1820s, the last house on the old road in the village on the way to Lincoln is Dial Cottage, so named for the sun dial seen on the ornate gable end in this photograph, c. 1900.

We finish our journey with this card and its poignant message sent by a soldier training at the nearby army camp during the First World War. In 1917 Fred Cunningham posted it home to his family in Tonbridge, Kent. After relating everyday occurrences and asking them to send him a letter he tells his mother there is no need for her to worry as he has just heard that there will be no more drafts going to France from his battalion. Just one of many thousands of similar cards sent all over the country from soldiers serving their country during this time of war. Let's hope that Fred had got his facts right and that he was to return safe and sound to his home in southern England.

Other local titles published by The History Press

Around Grantham
FRED LEADBETTER

This fascinating collection of more than 200 photographs and postcards will appeal to anyone with an interest in Grantham's history over the last century. Containing photographs taken by several of the most notable local photographers and starting at South Witham on the Rutland and Lincolnshire border, the reader is taken on a nostalgic journey up the ancient Great North Road, through Grantham and all the way to Long Bennington.
0 7524 1863 7

Haunted Lincolnshire
DANIEL CODD

This collection of stories contains well-known and new spooky tales from around the counties of Lincolnshire, North Lincolnshire and North-East Lincolnshire. From spectral monks at Lincoln's medieval cathedral and the highwayman who wanders the old coach yard of the fourteenth-century White Hart Hotel to the Green Lady of Thorpe Hall and the demon dog known as Black Shuck, this phenomenal gathering of ghostly goings-on is bound to captivate anyone interested in the supernatural history of the area.
0 7524 3817 4

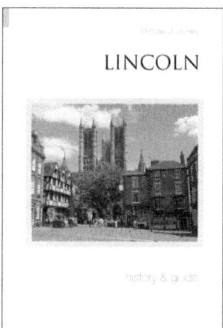

Lincoln: History and Guide
MICHAEL J. JONES

Lincoln was a major city under Roman, Viking, and medieval rule and each of these eras has left its mark on the city. Including a series of walking tours that show how the history of the city can be read in its existing streets and buildings, this book is a well-illustrated and readable introduction to the city's past that will appeal to residents and visitors alike.
0 7524 3389 X

Stamford and Surroundings
BRIAN ANDREWS

Stamford was once decribed as 'the finest stone-built town in England'. Characterised by limestone buildings and crooked stone-slated roofs, this selection of over 200 photographs ranges from images of the magnificent Burghley House to the humble stone cottages of the outlying villages, George V's coronation celebrations to the town's ancient local fair. *Stamford and Surroundings* provides a nostalgic tour of the area and details the history, and most importantly, the people who worked and played in this historic market town.
0 7524 3845 X

If you are interested in purchasing other books published by The History Press, or in case you have difficulty finding any of our books in your local bookshop, you can also place orders directly through our website
www.thehistorypress.co.uk